Raising Resilience

A Mother's Journey to Rediscovering Self Among Struggles

Tracy Holmes

ISBN: 978-1-915502-98-8. All rights reserved. © 2025 Tracy Holmes

All intellectual property rights including copyright, design right and publishing rights rest with the author. No part of this book may be reproduced or transmitted in any way including any written, electronic, recording, or photocopying without written permission of the author. This publication is a personal memoir from the author and views expressed are her own. Published in Ireland by Orla Kelly Publishing.

Orla Kelly Publishing
27 Kilbrody,
Mount Oval,
Rochestown,
Cork,
Ireland.

DISCLAIMER

The issues covered in this book derive directly from personal experience and does not constitute medical advice or endorse medical treatments or any other claims. Children's Health Ireland, Children's Health Foundation and staff have not participated in the development, writing or production of this book, which has been written independently by the author. Children's Health Ireland does not endorse any claim, medical advice, or other content of this publication and has not approved or substantiated same. Children's Health Ireland, Children's Health Foundation and staff will not receive any proceeds or other gratuity from the sale of this book. Any named Children's Health Ireland staff member has provided their consent to be named. The National Maternity Hospital have also not participated in the development or writing of this book and will not receive any proceeds of same. Any named staff of The National Maternity Hospital have provided their consent to be named. *Note some names used within this book have been changed to protect privacy.

For my boys,
Thank you for making me a mama and being my greatest teachers in life.

Prologue

"Why are you sitting on the floor?" Andrew asked, as the worry spread across his face.

There was a bed and a chair on offer, I could have had my choice, but it was the floor that called me. My body needed to feel the ground right now.

"I don't know," I shrugged, wondering how to tell my husband just how broken I felt.

Before my thoughts could gather themselves, I began to cry.

"I just can't do any of this anymore, Andrew," I sobbed, keeping my eyes on the floor, as Andrew sat down next to me. "I am just too exhausted; physically and mentally. My heart breaks every time I walk into that ward and see Freddie there. I'm failing on all fronts. I can't even give Theo a bottle for crying out loud! I don't have any energy left to be the mother I want to be. It's just all too much."

"We need to get that second opinion," he whispered, wrapping his arms around me.

The thought of going to *that* hospital – a mental health hospital – terrified me. All sorts of thoughts intruded my mind and I couldn't stop them.

"Would they think I'm a terrible mother?"
"Would they think I'm an unfit mother?"
"Would they try to take my kids from me?"
"Would they admit me against my will?"

Truth is, I didn't know what to expect and never in my wildest dreams did I think I would be considering visiting such a place; yet here we were.

As the thoughts continued to race through my mind like a bullet train, I felt my breathing rising and rising until I was struggling to catch up with its pace. My hands started to tingle and my head felt dizzy. I could hear Andrew talking to me but I wasn't taking in his words. I was so focused on catching my breath that I couldn't focus on anything except the white double-doors of the wardrobe in front of me. I inspected every part of it like it was the first time I had seen it. I was focusing, I needed to focus.

"Tracy, answer me!" Andrew demanded, the panic in his voice snapping me back.

"I think I just had a panic attack," I whispered.

I had never had a panic attack before so I'm not quite sure how I knew at that moment that it was one.

"Jesus, I thought you were going to pass out," Andrew sighed, before a strength took him. "Right! We are going to the hospital. Now!"

I didn't disagree; instead, I picked myself up off the floor, walked down the stairs and into the passenger seat of my car; not even acknowledging Beth or my boys as I did so.

Chapter 1

"Please appear, please appear, please…" I wished out loud, as I waited for a second blue line to appear on the pregnancy test. "We want this so much! Harry would make an amazing big brother. C'mon test, let's make him one."

Andrew and I met at work in 2010, when we were both in our early twenties. We worked for an Irish food retail company called Avoca that had multiple locations around the country. I'd worked for them since I was a teenager. It was my first part-time job while I was in school and after going on to study business and events in college, I worked my way up to management level.

Before meeting Andrew, I had moved from my home in Wicklow up north to Belfast to manage the food retail side of that location. I had the time of my life living up in Belfast, it was my first time living away from home and I relished in my newfound independence. My friend Aoife had also moved up with the company, so we shared an apartment together and spent our days working and evenings out exploring all Belfast had to offer. I felt free, independent, alive!

In January 2010, after being in Belfast for nearly a year, I reluctantly asked to be placed back down south for a couple of months. After being married for 26 years, my parents had decided to get a divorce and I felt I should come home to support my mum alongside my siblings, Niamh and Danny.

* * *

A few weeks later, I was back in Wicklow and settling into my new temporary post at a branch I'd never worked in before. Whatever was going on at home could always be paused as soon as I walked into work. It was my happy place, even the gloomy Irish weather couldn't stifle the love I had for my job.

"Muffin?" signalled the head chef, as he gestured baked goods my way. He was 6ft with a mop of sandy-brown hair that had a slight curl to it. He was good-looking, a bit young to be a head-chef I thought, but then again, I got that all the time too being a manager at only 22.

"Oh, sorry, what?" I mumbled, as I tried not to talk with my mouth full of lunch.

"Want a muffin? They're banana and walnut. I'm trying out a new recipe. I'm Andrew, by the way," he clarified, even though we'd already been introduced.

"Oh lovely, yes please. They smell delicious. I'm Tracy," I nodded, both cool as cucumbers here.

We sat out in the cold, the artificial heat beaming on us from the heater above, sipping coffee and putting the world to rights. By the end of our break, we'd exchanged numbers and had agreed to go on date.

Andrew says he knew from that moment that we'd be together; I was more sceptical. Meeting Andrew led me to an emotional crossroads. On one hand, I knew there was something special about this guy and I knew I wanted to find out more. On the other hand, I was witnessing first-hand the end of a marriage, which had survived over two decades and three children. How does that suddenly all go wrong, how do you come back from that? And more importantly, why would you put yourself through all of that for it just to collapse around you? Surely the risk wasn't worth it.

Despite all those worries, I very quickly realized that our paths were meant to cross and we didn't look back after that first date. He was my calm during a time of my life that was utter chaos and 14 years later, he still remains my grounding influence, my safe place, my home. Loving Andrew taught me that the risk of being vulnerable and putting your heart on the line is worth it.

As planned after things were more stable at home, I moved back to Belfast after three months and we made it work. We both loved our jobs and were very career-driven so we respected that and encouraged each other to drive forward at work. I came home to Wicklow in 2011 and in 2012 we moved in together. In 2013, Andrew set up an outdoor food catering business specializing in weddings and a year later, after it took off quickly, I left my job and joined him running the back end of the business and the front-of-house at the events. It seemed like a natural progression for us, we had exhausted what we wanted to achieve within our current roles, so it made sense as the next step. We worked long hours getting it off the ground and building our reputation, but we loved every minute of it.

Our lifestyle for the next few years was the epitome of work hard, play hard. We put blood, sweat and tears into the business but outside it we enjoyed date nights, socializing with friends and the occasional holiday.

* * *

"Excuse me, would you mind taking a picture of us?" Andrew asked an American tourist who was sat next to us. We were coming to the end of our two-week visit to Thailand in 2015 and soaking up the views on our sunset cruise around Phuket.

"Sure, no problem," she replied, as I watched her take the camera from Andrew, before he returned to me.

We were anchored in the middle of the sea watching the sun so big and bright it looked like an enormous fireball sinking lower and lower towards the sea as I suddenly heard a gasp escape from the camera-wielding tourist. I looked up and followed her gaze back down to Andrew, who was now on his knee, with a ring in his hand.

"Tracy Luckie, will you marry me?" Andrew confidently asked, beaming ear to ear.

"Yes! Yes! Yes!" I fell into his arms. Yes! I hadn't thought too much about how or when Andrew might propose but this, the way he chose to do it, was far beyond my wildest expectations and a moment I knew I would treasure forever.

And a little over a year later, on a wet day in March which was a stark contrast to the day we got engaged, although just as magical, I married the love of my life.

* * *

We hadn't talked much about having kids before we got married, we were both so career-driven that we spent more time talking about our hopes and dreams in that department than about starting a family. It would also be fair to say that I wouldn't describe myself as a very maternal person, the burning desire to become a mother was never really there but I knew Andrew always saw us having kids down the line, so it was something I always knew we would get to at some point - when the time was right.

After our wedding, we went to Italy for 10 days. It was on this trip that we talked more in-depth about having kids. We agreed that we didn't want a big family but we also didn't want to have an only child so, if we were lucky enough to, we would like two children.

"Andrew, you know me by now, you know how important my job is to me," I gingerly explained.

"For sure, and you know how important it is to me too," he replied.

"Yes, but things can be a little different for women. Or there can be an assumption there, when it wouldn't be for men," I needed to say what I needed to say. I could feel it brewing.

"Okay, what assumption?" Andrew asked, quizzically.

"That if I want kids, I'll want to give up my job and be a stay-at-home mum," I began. "But the thing is, that's never going to be me, Andrew. I want to continue growing in my career, it's a non-negotiable for me. My job is that important. So, we'll need to factor in childcare costs when we do have kids, because I'll be working just as much as you are."

"You worried me for a second there," Andrew answered, relieved. "Of course, I never expected anything else!"

It definitely made me nervous to think about becoming a mother. It seemed like a huge responsibility and after gaining so much independence in my 20s I felt scared to lose that. But after our engagement, I did soften towards the idea, creating a human that was half me and half Andrew, knowing who he or she might be, was something I found myself thinking about more as time went on. So, after our honeymoon, we decided that we'd start trying to have our first baby after busy season at work that November.

* * *

To my surprise, I got pregnant very quickly and in August 2018, during an Irish heatwave, Harry was born. I will never forget that summer, I had managed to work the whole pregnancy with no complications but during those final weeks, heavily pregnant and swollen in the sweltering heat, I had a whole new level of appreciation for women and what our bodies can do, it was the greatest challenge of my life up to that point.

We were besotted with Harry, named after my late-grandfather whom I unfortunately never got to meet, from the moment he was born. Swept up in that glorious newborn bubble it felt like he was always here and life before him never existed.

"You are the sweetest little boy I have ever met," I cooed to my newborn. Andrew and our families had headed home for the night, and I got to spend my first hours alone with Harry. "I am going to love you to the moon and back."

As the hormones of the labour continued to flush through my system, I could feel my body fill up with emotions. Like my blood had been replaced by feelings, running through my veins. The rush of love was indescribable. How could I feel so much for this little being already. How is that possible?

Suddenly, sitting here in the busy postnatal ward with the air hot and heavy and various different babies' coos and cries softened by the light hushing of their mama behind the thin blue curtains that separated each of us, I was hit by the jolt of a realization. It hit me so hard I felt physically winded.

"My life is no longer my own," I thought, as the weight in my arms became heavier. "This tiny little soul is now MY responsibility."

My mind started to spiral.

"Andrew and I can never just decide to go to the cinema on a whim again," I thought. Of course, this wasn't true, my deliriously tired and emotional postpartum self had clearly never heard of a babysitter! That said, I knew this shift in self was bigger than I'd expected. I wasn't quite sure how much bigger, but I could feel the responsibilities start to stack up.

While I was pregnant, I also naively thought I could cope with a newborn and continue to do my work with no downtime. I remember bouncing on my yoga ball in the pre-labour ward sending a contract to a new wedding client between contractions, that's how high up on my priority list work was.

I was soon sharply brought back to earth as sleepless nights, breastfeeding struggles, colic and reflux made their presence felt and taught me to slow down and embrace this time. This was life now, we had a baby and life wouldn't be the same again, sacrifices needed to be made.

So that's what I did, for the first time in 15 years I didn't put work first. I leaned on support to cover some of my duties and although I continued working a bit, I massively cut-back and enjoyed our version of maternity leave with Harry.

We spent our days at mum and baby groups, going for walks or meeting friends for lunch and then during naptimes and in evenings when Harry would go to bed, I would work. I was blessed, he loved his sleep; he takes after his mama there.

When Harry was 9 months old, we hired a childminder. I found that harder than I thought I would, I had come to love our days together and the bond we had but I knew I would always be a working mum. Once he went to his minder, I felt like life was levelling out again and I found balance. Andrew and I even squeezed in the odd trip to the cinema!

* * *

Not long later, in the summer of 2019, we started having discussions around having another child to complete our little family. These conversations made me nervous, making those sacrifices again, all the while already having a son who at that time felt like our whole world – that wasn't a decision to be taken lightly. The business was also much bigger at this point too, we were six years in and were booking out for weddings 12 to 18 months in advance. We had just bought our first home, in Andrew's hometown of Greystones, in Wicklow, and were also on the cusp of opening our first delicatessen and had a staff of 10 people relying on us for employment. All of that felt like pressure. Such big pressure.

That pressure didn't lift until September 2020, when we eventually decided to try for number two. We were mid-pandemic and even though that was scary in itself, we were lucky that our work was stable but a bit quieter than usual.

Back in March 2020 when the world came to a halt, our business dried up overnight as weddings were cancelled after lockdowns tried to stop the virus spreading. That financial worry was terrifying and we didn't know what this meant for the future but we were extremely lucky that our delicatessen, Kitchen 28, was already up and running and as a take-out eatery, so we were allowed to continue to trade under government guidelines. The deli saved us, and our business, during what would go on to be over a year of no weddings. So it was during this quieter period that it felt like a better time than any to hopefully expand our family.

On 4 December 2020, that second blue line did appear and we were excited about welcoming our new addition. We decided to keep the news to ourselves for Christmas, have an early scan in January and go from there.

* * *

In January, we booked an early scan in a private clinic. I was about 8 weeks pregnant and had no reason to be concerned, but I am a hugely impatient person and wanted to know how our new little one was doing. I remember driving to the scan on a gloomy Saturday afternoon with Andrew and feeling the faintest flutter in my tummy. "I must have imagined that," I thought, and quickly turned to Dr Google for answers: 'Some pregnant women expecting multiples can feel flutters as early as 8 weeks' the first article read. "Multiples? Ha, imagine. My mind must be playing tricks on me," I thought, as we headed into our scan.

Lying on the bed in the dimly-lit room of the clinic with soft music playing lightly in the background, the abrupt cold shock of the jelly on my belly made me shudder as we kept our eyes glued to the screen waiting to see our little bean.

"There is the sac and there is the heartbeat," our sonographer said in a thick American accent.

Immediately I let out a sigh, those initial seconds of waiting to 'hear' my baby were dauting, hoping and praying that amongst the black and grey haze on the screen, a little flicker indicating a heartbeat would be there. I'd been nervous, worrying about miscarriage, knowing that one in four women do. So, relief filled my lungs when I heard that little heartbeat. I celebrated quietly, afraid to speak too loudly and scare it away, all the while holding on to every fibre of hope that our little bean sticks and holds on.

"And here is the second sac and heartbeat," she said.

"What?!" we both said rather loudly in unison as our heads flew in her direction.

The sonographer gave us a beaming smile and she said those three life-changing words, "it's twins, congratulations!"

I don't know what I felt in that moment, I was just dumbfounded. Twins, wow! The sonographer went on to tell us she was a twin and it's amazing, they will have a bond like no other. I regarded her comment by returning the smile and nod I knew she was expecting, when really, I could feel the beginnings of tears start to sting at my eyes.

We went through the motions for the rest of the scan, myself and Andrew occasionally giving each other a side-eye glance that we both silently knew meant "What. The. Fuck?!"

After getting our images and exchanging pleasantries with

the sonographer, we left and sat mostly in silence on the way home except for muttering the odd "oh my god".

That night in bed I cried to Andrew; "I'm happy they're ok, but twins! How will we cope?"

"Lots of people have twins and cope, we will too" Andrew said, his calm level-headedness coming into gear.

There were so many thoughts to process and navigate though, my mind felt dizzy from the thoughts coming thick and fast like a tornado.

"We only planned for two kids, three was not in our plan."

"We'll need a bigger car."

"I can forget going back to work full-time, childcare for three kids will be insane!"

"I don't want to be a stay-at-home mum; I want the career too."

"How will I make any time for Harry with TWO newborns!"

"How will I cope with TWO newborns?!"

"What have we done?"

I went to sleep with the weight of the world on my shoulders, this was big and I wasn't sure how to begin to even start unpacking the mental load of it all. All the memories of those first few weeks after Harry's birth flew to the forefront of my mind as if it were yesterday. Trying to imagine living through that reality again, times two, and with a toddler in tow. It felt like a mountain too steep to climb.

* * *

The following weeks passed by spent in a haze of worry and nervous-anticipation but eventually the mental load felt a little lighter. Maybe I had just needed some time to let it sink in or maybe it's because everything can seem so much worse when you are in a state of shock, whatever the reason as the weeks went by, I just knew we would make it work; we would have to. These were our babies and despite our reservations they were loved and wanted.

As I navigated my way through the feelings and emotions, and the pregnancy nausea that had now made its presence felt, guilt also set in. Lots of women long and pray for babies and struggle, no doubt receiving the news of twins would bring undeniable joy to many women, so why was I not one of them? I was so ungrateful. I had some friends who had miscarried, some who had multiple miscarriages. I tried to put myself in their shoes, impossible as that is as I wouldn't even try to imagine how heartbreaking that loss can feel, but I would think a twin pregnancy would bring so much joy after the trauma of a loss. We may be having three children over the two we pictured but weren't we lucky? Our babies were growing and were healthy, I was feeling good for the most part and we had a happy and healthy two-year-old at home. We were so lucky. Perspective is so powerful and perspective is what I found in that moment. Another thing was for sure, Harry would be in his element with two siblings, I just knew he would make the best big brother.

We went on to tell our families and closest friends, all of whom were so delighted and excited for us. I look back now and I am so thankful for their reactions, our babies deserved to be celebrated from the start and I still hold guilt that I let fear takeover; I am so happy and grateful that others gave us that gift.

On 11 March 2021, on our fourth wedding anniversary, we went for another private scan to find out the genders. My routine 20-week scan at the hospital was coming up a couple of weeks later but due to covid restrictions I knew Andrew wouldn't be allowed to attend and we wanted to find out the genders together. I always knew it would be two boys, and I was right. Maybe it was mothers' intuition or maybe it was because Harry was a boy that I had now self-labelled myself as a "boy-mom" but either way, I just couldn't picture one, or both, of them being girls.

We were really happy to be having boys and two brothers for Harry, we told Harry first and then told my family. We didn't want a big gender reveal, it wasn't us, but we did want to do something fun to tell the family and have Harry involved so we went to the shop and asked him to pick two blue things to show his nana, aunt, uncle and cousins he was having two brothers. He picked two blue slush-puppies, would you expect anything less? He was literally a kid in a sweet shop! So that's how our families found out, two blue slushies and a 2-year-old with a VERY blue tongue - and a major sugar rush!

In the weeks and months that followed, we continued with normal life while gradually getting ready for our home to soon be filled with two new people. It is crazy how something so small can take up so much room, especially two of them. Harrys' cot came out of the attic and we purchased a second, a double buggy and two highchairs, soon leaving little room for much else. The house suddenly started to feel much smaller than it had a few weeks earlier.

I noticed how this pregnancy was also so different from my first, I was much bigger, much sooner and really struggled to keep up with an energetic and boisterous two-year-old. It really made me reflect on my first pregnancy and I came to the realisation that you'll never experience pregnancy for the first-time again, a time when you can be totally selfish and lean into the slowing-down and self-care more than you can on subsequent pregnancies. I suddenly regretted that I didn't take more time to enjoy it first-time round and put my feet up more.

I was then met with new feeling I never anticipated to feel: anxiety. Anxiety about how I would navigate mothering two new babies, while still giving my sweet first-born all the love and nurturing he needs. I find it hard to explain my love for Harry, I feel his birth created a rebirth in me. Yes, those initial couple of months were hard, but he opened my eyes to a world of love I had never experienced before, and I knew I would go to the ends of the earth to protect him. That feeling makes me feel so vulnerable, the fear that sometimes you might not be able to protect them from what this crazy world can throw at us, and that fear can take your breath away sometimes.

I confided these feelings I was having to a friend of mine, Lisa, who was pregnant on her first baby and we were due only a week apart. I told her I was struggling with these emotions and fearful I couldn't love another human being as much as I loved Harry.

"Have you heard of the term 'matrescence'?" she asked.

"No, what's that?" I replied intrigued.

"It's the process of becoming a mother," she explained. "It's the physical, psychological and emotional changes we go through when we give birth to a child. This is what you're going through right now."

This was a revelation to me, there was a word for what I had felt, and was feeling, and not only that, I wasn't alone. The more I thought of it though, the more it made sense. Of course, we wouldn't be the same, we go through this huge, life-altering transition how could we expect to remain the same person? As I digested that, I came to the thinking that women who become mothers are like two people, we get two lives. Until we become a mother, we are women with our own identity and values, some of us may go through harder times that others, some of us may experience illness, loss or grief, some of us may live vibrant and carefree lives but once that rebirth happens, we will never be the same. It's like we are cracked open from the core, raw and vulnerable and we experience a type of love and protective instincts we couldn't have ever imagined. Our values change, our priorities change and suddenly every decision we go on to make will be made with another person in mind. Why weren't we talking about this more? Why weren't we shouting this loud for those in the back to hear?

As I entered the sixth month of my pregnancy and with this new understanding of matrescence, I really tried to be kinder to myself and trust that what I was feeling was normal and okay. I had a lot of anxiety about carrying twins as the weeks passed, I could definitely feel that 'twin one' was a lot more active than 'twin two', so I found myself making fairly regular trips to the maternity hospital for check-ups. Every time I went in and had a scan, everything looked fine but I just couldn't shake the feeling something was wrong.

One evening after yet another trip to the hospital where I was reassured, I came home to put Harry to bed. Afterwards I came downstairs and burst into tears.

"What's wrong?" Andrew comforted, rushing to my side. "Are you feeling okay? Are the babies okay?"

I tried to reassure him between breathless sobs that it wasn't the babies, it was me.

"I don't think I deserve to be having twins," I shared, nervously, sobbing uncontrollably as I did. "I spent so long in the beginning feeling sad about having two babies, I let the practicalities of life overshadow the emotions of what should have been a really happy time."

"Hun, you were just dealing with the shock of the double whammy. That was a natural response," he tried to reassure me. "Of course you deserve to have them!"

"But if something is wrong with one or both of them, then it'll be my fault, because I spent so much time only wanting to have one," I cried.

Truth was, I had come to bond with these boys, both of them. They were very much wanted and loved and I had started to picture what life would look like with them. Would they look like each other? Would they look like Harry? Would they have similar personalities or be wildly different? I became excited to meet them and start this new chapter, but every time I got excited, I would be stopped in my tracks, guilt rearing its ugly head again. I didn't deserve these boys, echoing over and over.

Andrew managed to calm me down, "we deserve these babies" he said, "you are the best mum and these boys are lucky to have you, let yourself be excited. It's okay."

I tried to let his words sink in and I tried to relax into my last trimester but I was also well aware of the risk with twins and early delivery. That fact alone wasn't ideal when you run your own business, and I started to worry about what would happen in my absence, especially if the boys did come early and need to be in a neonatal unit for a while. I needed Andrew to be by my side but ultimately if I had to step out of the business it meant leaving even more on his plate.

I shared these fears with Andrew and we agreed that we should hire someone for a year's maternity leave cover so that I didn't have to worry about the business and could focus on my own well-being and that of the boys. It would also mean that Andrew would continue to have that support system in work.

We both knew I would never be able to take a year off, especially given my independent streak, but at least this gave us time and space to adjust to our new world and I could ease myself back in when I felt ready.

My due date was 18 August, coincidently the exact same due date as Harry three years previous. So, we decided to hire someone right away so I could do a month's handover and technically finish up at the end of May. That would give me time to do as much or as little work as I wanted while preparing for the boys' arrival and spending some precious time with Harry while we were still our little unit of three. If the boys did come early, we'd be prepared.

I was so organized, sometimes I think organization is woven in my DNA but the trouble with being too organized is that you are not prepared for things going off-course and losing control and when things go off-course, and if control is lost, everything can unravel.

Chapter 2

On 1 May, my replacement Laura started. I already felt lighter knowing Andrew and I now had a support system in place, knowing I could surrender to what was to come. In my true organized fashion, I had prepared a detailed schedule, I would do one month with Laura and finish up on 28 May, this gave us ten or so weeks before the twins arrived, which I felt was a comfortable timeframe. More importantly, it would also give me some time to rest and start nesting at home, which I was itching to begin.

"Right, it's 3pm, I'm just going to start saying goodbye to some people," I told Andrew, as my last day of work wrapped up. Four weeks had flown by and I was planning on a quiet exit, with a few hugs, before heading home for my much-needed time of nesting.

"That's a good idea. Before you do, I think Laura was looking for you in the kitchen," Andrew replied, ushering me out of the room and down the stairs.

"Surprise!" The team cheered, handing me flowers and gifts, each expecting a hug before I left. There was no chance for me to escape quietly, but I welcomed every second, as each wished us well on our next adventure. Suddenly, it all began to feel very real and I had mixed emotions about stepping away. On one hand, I was excited to focus on something other than work for a while, but on the other hand I was so nervous. It was the first time I'd ever given away any control in my work and that, for me, was scary. No matter how good your replacement is, as a business owner, you know nobody will care or do as well at the job as you do, and there was a level of anxious anticipation about how the coming months would go.

I went home that evening and after getting Harry to bed I decided to have an early night myself, while Andrew worked late at an event. As I got into my pyjamas, it dawned on me that I was suddenly struggling to see my feet under the blossoming bump, I was now bigger at 27 weeks pregnant with twins than I was at 38 weeks with Harry – all 8.4pound of him! I took a picture from the top of my belly downwards and posted it on Instagram: #hellomaternityleavegoodbyetoes.

I got into bed, my feet thanking me for the gesture, as I realized just how much this pregnancy was taking out of me. I don't know if it was because I had a really busy month doing the handover, or if it was because I was realizing just how different a twin pregnancy is to a singleton one, but I was absolutely exhausted - both physically and mentally. I had underestimated the mental capacity it can take when you are juggling so many balls in the air, my head was heavy and I knew it was time to let the load lighten.

We went on to have a lovely weekend at home, Andrew was off so we enjoyed some family time with Harry. On the Saturday night the both of us got out for a meal to celebrate my maternity leave and this new impending chapter.

"You know, we've kicked around so many names for the boys," Andrew admitted, while spooning gratin potato onto his plate accompanying his steak, "but I keep coming back to those two."

"Me too!" I replied, excited that we'd both agreed. "We've been calling them Twin One and Twin Two for so long, it'll be lovely to start calling them by their actual names. Even while we wait."

"Agreed!" Andrew smiled. "So, we're going with Theo for Twin One and Freddie for Twin Two."

We talked about how far we'd come since that day in January when we found out it was twins. Don't get me wrong, we were still nervous about what was in store, but we were excited now to meet our boys and witness Harry become a big brother.

It's only when you have one-on-one time together as a couple that you remember what it was like before you had children. It always amazes me how you can miss someone that you see every day but it's true, you do miss them. Not that we would change our life for the world, but when you embark on a journey to have a family you do have to have to let go of a part of your relationship you once had, the part where you were each other's whole world.

Truth is, you now have to accept that there are other people in your relationship and you both know that the little person who has entered your world becomes higher on your priority list than each other. It can be sad to come to that realization, and like most things in life you only realize it once you have experienced it. I wondered how we would make time for each other once there were three little ones in our life.

* * *

A few days later, on Tuesday 1 June, we headed into the hospital for a routine scan. As it was a twin pregnancy, I was having routine growth scans every week from 26 weeks. Our boys were fraternal twins, each with their own sac and placenta, non-identical. Twins that are identical are called monozygotic twins and they are two babies who share the same sac and placenta. The risk of twins slowing in growth is typically more common in monozygotic twins than in fraternal twins, as they have to fight harder for space and nutrients. As our babies had their own placentas, this was less likely but any twin pregnancy is a higher risk than a singleton, so keeping a closer eye on growth is generally normal practice in the third trimester.

It was a warm sunny morning in Dublin as we headed into the hospital, the first signs of summer making its presence felt. Andrew was off work, so himself and Harry came to the hospital with me that morning. Of course, due to covid restrictions, they weren't allowed in, so Andrew planned to bring Harry to the park and playground across the road and I'd meet them after for lunch.

At my appointment, I was lying on the bed going through the usual chatter that I was so accustomed to at this point I could nearly say it in my sleep.

"Twins, yes."

"No, twins don't run in the family."

"No, it wasn't IVF, it was spontaneous."

"Yes, a two-and-a-half-year-old at home."

"Yes, 3 under 3, it's going be chaos!"

We went through the usual rigmarole. They'd start with twin one and do all the checks – heart rate, length, head circumference, estimated weight and so forth. Thankfully all continued to look good there. Theo was definitely going to be the leader of the pack, I thought, he was always so active and loved keeping me up at night already.

As I relaxed into the scan, it was on to twin two. She noted the heart rate was good as she swiftly moved onto the length checks. She spent longer this time, dragging the curser from one end of the leg to the other, then starting again.

"Is everything ok?" I asked.

"It could just be the way baby is lying, but I am not entirely happy with some of my measurements so I am going to get another nurse to have a look," she replied, concerned.

She popped out of the room to get a colleague while I lay and waited, my heart was pounding in my chest. The room suddenly felt chilly and more clinical than it had five minutes previous. As the second sonographer did her checks, I knew there was no error, there was a problem here.

"Twin one, as you know is growing as expected," the original sonographer reiterated, calmly. Good news, before bad, I thought. "But twin two is not. His femur length is shorter than it should be for 28 weeks."

"What does this mean?" I asked, feeling very alone and unprepared for any bad news.

"We are going to send you for a doppler scan," she replied. "This will check the placenta and how that's functioning. Your husband can join you for that scan, if you want him there." This made me even more nervous as I willed myself internally to stay calm.

"Andrew, can you talk?" I asked as soon as he picked up the call, making sure he hadn't put me on speakerphone for Harry to hear.

"Yep," he replied, his usual upbeat humour not sensing the worry in my voice.

"They said twin two, I mean Freddie, isn't growing like he should. And I have to go for another scan today. It's called a doppler scan. They said you can join me for this one, which scared me. Why would they suggest that?" I let the words tumble out of my mouth.

"I'm sure everything is going to be okay," he calmed me. "They'd probably know something different than normal would put you under stress, so they're letting me be there to relieve that."

"You're right, that makes sense," I said, relieved. My grounded husband calming my concerns as always.

"I've got Harry, though," he mentioned, "but I'll call my parents and ask if they can drive in and watch him for us. It'll be about 40 minutes before they get here, but I'll text you when they're on their way."

"Thank you, see you soon," I replied, grateful that our families were so willing to help.

Those 40 minutes felt like the longest wait and time was not something I wanted more of right now. Time allowed me too much space to be in my head and start catastrophizing. But finally, Andrew popped his head in the waiting room door, and we headed down the corridor for the doppler scan.

As we entered the ultrasound room for a second time, we were greeted by a kindly smiling sonographer called Mel. You know sometimes you just think people are made to do a job? Well, I felt she was meant to be looking after me on this day. She spoke softly and calmly and really did her best to put me at ease. As she manoeuvred her way around my belly, she told me she was going to focus on the placenta, twin one was fine but twin two was showing signs of a slower placenta function.

I was confused, she could have been speaking Spanish for all I knew, as I struggled to understand what she was trying to say. The confusion must have been evident on my face as she went on to dumb it down for us.

"As you can see here, twin one's placenta is going beat, beat, beat, consistently. When we look at twin two, his placenta is going beat, beat, skip, beat," Mel explained, simplifying what felt like important information.

"This means twin two's placenta isn't functioning to 100% and would explain his slowing of growth. I'm going to get a multiples specialist to come speak to us. I'll be back shortly."

As she left the room, I broke down, burying myself into Andrew's arms. Was this the start of it? I knew I would be punished for only wanting two children, maybe I was getting my just deserts, I thought to myself.

As promised, a specialist came to speak to us a while later and explained more in detail what was happening. He said it was called *placenta insufficiency* and although it was not hugely common, it was serious. He went on to tell us that once a placenta becomes insufficient it doesn't right itself, so early delivery would most likely happen. He couldn't give an exact reason for what was causing the insufficiency, or if it would continue to slow further, but said ongoing monitoring was essential.

In that moment, I felt a little robbed. I had only just started my maternity leave; this was meant to be the start of me enjoying some downtime before our life would drastically change. This news would obviously mean more visits to the hospital, eating up my time at home. I would soon realize that would have been the ideal scenario, after what he was about to say next.

"We need to admit you today and you will need to stay here until you deliver the babies," he said, so casually that our jaws dropped.

Shit.

This was not good.

I was told to go home and pack a bag and be back in before 6pm that evening to be admitted. We'd then go over the plan of what to expect but the gist of it was that I would have daily doppler scans and I would hopefully get to 34 weeks when they would then perform a c-section to deliver the boys.

We drove home in a haze, I struggled to process all this new information. This wasn't how this day was meant to go. At this moment we were meant to be sitting across the road in the park showing Harry the blurry ultrasound pictures of his brothers, not driving home to essentially move into the hospital for the next six weeks. As that thought hit me, it took my breath away.

"I can't do it, Andrew. I can't live in the hospital away from my you and Harry, I won't cope without you and you won't cope with Harry on your own with work too. I told you this would happen! I told you something wasn't right and I would be punished for only wanting one baby!" I sobbed, hard.

"Tracy! This is not your fault. Get that out of your head right now!" Andrew demanded. "Everything will be ok; we just need to take things a day at a time" he said more softly as he squeezed my knee reassuringly.

The thought of a c-section also terrified me. Naturally, I knew it was a possibility but I had really hoped and believed I could deliver these babies vaginally as I had done Harry. This wasn't what I wanted; this can't be happening.

Andrew's parents had brought Harry home after they came in to collect him the couple of hours previous.

"Is everything ok? Andrews mum Beth asked cautiously with a look of worry etched across her face, as we walked into the kitchen where they were all seated.

I started to well up as the silence lingered in the room.

"Come on son, let's go into the garden" Paul, Andrew's dad, said to Harry as he ushered him out our back double-doors, sensing it was a conversation not for him to overhear.

"There is a problem with twin twos growth and Tracy needs to be admitted today so they can keep an eye on things" Andrew explained. It was strange to hear Andrew say twin two after we had been so used to calling him Freddie for the last few days but we hadn't shared our boys' names with family yet wanting to keep it as a surprise considering everyone already knew we were having two boys.

"Oh love, I am so sorry. What can we do to help?" Beth asked softly as she rubbed my back.

"Please just support Andrew and Harry, I will be looked after in there. I need to know Harry will be ok, this is going to be hard on him" I whispered fighting back more sobs.

I knew I didn't even need to ask this of them, Andrew was extremely close to his parents, they were both retirees in their early seventies, not that you'd know it given how active and full of life they both were. Paul is an ex-firefighter who still walks by the sea every day and plays golf a couple of times a week and Beth swims every morning and has a social calendar that would make a teenager jealous! I felt so privileged to be a part of their family, they were such good people. After my parents' divorce 12 years ago, we were estranged from my dad, so he was no longer in our family structure; it had been a difficult time initially but I had made peace with that now. And with the absence of my own father in my life for my adult years, I had become very close to my father-in-law and now saw him as a father too. They also absolutely adored Harry, who was their first grandchild, and at the tender age of only two, Harry knew just how to pull at his grandads heartstrings and get exactly what he wanted!

"Of course we will love. Just focus on yourself and those babies, we have everything under control here" Beth exclaimed confidently making my shoulders drop a little with relief.

After packing up a bag, we made our way back to the hospital, where they allowed Andrew in until I was admitted and settled. The consultant on duty came to see us and told us the plan. Every day I would have a doppler scan, they would book me in with Mel on her days on duty as the continuity of one person who is familiar with what they are looking at day-on-day can make a difference. I would also have twice-daily traces to listen in to the babies' movements and heartbeats. She said that later that evening they also wanted to give me a steroid injection, this injection would help boost the babies' lungs should they need to be delivered early. And I if I made it another two weeks along, they would give another injection then. She said I wasn't high-risk for a spontaneous labour as there was no worry of my waters breaking early and being open to infection, so for that reason, I was allowed leave the hospital for walks, to meet family outside etc. This felt like the first glimmer of hope since I entered that ultrasound room this morning. After the consultant left, I told Andrew to go home to Harry, we knew the plan now and we agreed we'd talk in the morning.

* * *

After Andrew left, a midwife named Anna came to do my observations. I took one look at her and I couldn't believe it. One of my good traits is that I never forget a name or a face, and this midwife standing in front of me was Anna - the midwife who delivered Harry. I asked her if it was her, I told her it was August 2018 and she said she was working the delivery ward then, so yes, it was her.

"I'm so scared, Anna," I immediately confessed. "This is nothing like my first pregnancy. My hopes and dreams for a similar birthing experience feel like they're slipping away".

She put her hand on my shoulder and said, "I am sorry you are here, but we will look after you now."

And that was it, the straw that broke the camel's back, I sobbed like a baby, as Anna tried her best to console me. The same arms that, almost three years previous, wrapped me in a hug and congratulated me on the birth of our first-born baby boy were the same arms comforting me now as I sat in despair, fearful for my second-born sons' welfare. How funny life can be, but I chose to think of it as a positive sign and to believe everything would be ok. It had to be.

Surprisingly, I actually managed to get good night's sleep that night, the heaviness that all the crying created meant I fell into a deep slumber. I spoke with Andrew on the phone the next morning, he had spent the previous evening making plans with my mum and sister, his parents, and our childminder to organize care for Harry around his work and we agreed they would both come see me every second evening - every day was too much to ask.

"Mama, I had cocopops for breakfast!" Harry bellowed down the phone.

"Chocolate for breakfast on a Wednesday! Daddy is naughty!" I mocked.

"It's just a little treat for today, isn't it Harry?" Andrew exclaimed.

"We will see" Harry said cheekily evoking roars of laughter out of his mum and dad.

"How are you this morning?" Andrew asked softly.

"Better" I said, and surprisingly, I meant it.

I decided I needed to use this time wisely, just because I was in hospital didn't mean I couldn't choose to relax and wind down. Yes, it was a scary time, I didn't know what the next few weeks would bring, but I knew remaining as calm as I could would only go in my favour and be more beneficial to the twins than me freaking out and stressing. I questioned on some subconscious level did I know this would happen? Since April, I had felt deep in my gut that we needed to hire a replacement for the business and that I would finish up on 28 May. Did I know this was coming?

That night another woman was admitted to the bed beside me.

"Hey, I'm Leanne" she said cheerily the next morning as the midwife pulled back the curtain separating us.

"I'm Tracy" I smiled back. "How far along are you? I asked, my head nodding in gesture to her blossoming bump that looked full-term to me.

"I'm 31 weeks, I am having identical twins but one of them is taking more of the placenta than the other so I'm here" she shrugged.

"Oh my god, me too!" I exclaimed as I swung my legs over the bed to face her head on with genuine enthusiasm. "Well, mine aren't identical but one of my boys isn't growing as well as the other so I need to be here to be monitored more closely" I explained.

"Two boys? I am having two girls!" Leanne gushed.

"A ready-made foursome!" the midwife interjected cheekily making us both giggle.

"Congratulations. Are they your first?" I asked.

"Yep, you?" she replied.

"No, I have a two-and-a-half-year-old boy at home" I said softly. I almost didn't want to say it as I knew I would get sympathy in response and I also knew any kindness shown towards myself and Harry right now would open the floodgates.

"Jesus! Three boys! Your house is going to be mental!" Leanne said rather loudly.

I chuckled in response. I liked this girl.

We quickly struck up a bond and outside of chatting with our other halves on the phone or going out to meet them, we would spend our days and evenings chatting.

It really helped having that companionship with someone who understood at a time that was so hard. I think we were put together to pull each other through and that's just what we did. A couple of days later, another woman joined us called Lynn. She was having a baby boy and was having issues with her waters breaking early, she was on complete bedrest which I can appreciate must be so hard - I lived for my trips out of the hospital. Leanne and I would do our best to reassure Lynn and keep her spirits up.

The days that followed were a blur of routine, not my usual routine, but I guess this was my new-normal for now. In the morning after breakfast, I would go for my scan, with - for the most part - Mel, which really reassured me. She made me feel at ease during a time that was of total dis-ease. The doppler scan continued to show no improvement, in fact it was getting that little bit slower functioning every couple of days. This made me feel like such a bad mum, I felt like I was failing my baby boys. Why was my body not stepping up and coming through for these last few weeks? At times I wished they would just tell me that it was time for them to come out. Did that make me really selfish? I just wanted this to be over, I wanted to go home and deal with whatever was to come next. I wanted to be with Andrew and Harry, I was starting to feel so disconnected. I was trying my best to stay strong and positive but I was finding it incredibly tough. I hadn't spent more than two nights away from Harry since he was born so this was tough – the separation physically hurt.

I was a week into my stay when suddenly Leanne was told the news that it was time to get her babies out and she was going for a c-section. We had only known each other a week but it felt like much longer. When you spend so much time with a person in a confined space, coupled with that fact that you are going through a uniquely difficult time that only the other truly understands, you do become close - fast. I was nervous for Leanne but I was also sad for me, I was losing my ally and I found it hard to imagine how I would continue this journey without her. We exchanged phone numbers as we promised to stay in contact inside and outside this hospital and I knew we would both keep that promise.

"Good luck, mama. You've got this" I encouraged as I squeezed her hand before she was wheeled out of the ward and in the direction of the theatre.

A few hours later her boyfriend came up to tell myself and Lynn their two girls had made it safely into the world and were currently in the neonatal intensive care unit, NICU, getting a bit of support. Leanne was also doing well, which I was so relieved to hear.

* * *

That night I lay in bed, I poked and prodded by belly looking for my boys to keep me company. They dutifully answered my call in the form of kicks and jabs to the ribs. I had been thinking of middle names for the boys and I had come up with a couple.

"I was thinking James for Theo's middle name, what do you think?" I text to Andrew. It was a name I always liked and I felt it sat well after the name Theo. Andrew agreed and so we were decided.

"I don't know what goes well with Freddie but I think I would like his middle name to be Liam. It means strong-willed warrior and seems fitting for him given the circumstances" I text again to Andrew.

"Perfect," he replied. I felt at peace. Whatever was to come I knew our boy was fighting to be here and I would do everything I could to get him here safely.

The next day Leanne came up to visit myself and Lynn. She looked so well; I could see that new-mama glow all over her face. Lynn and I were like two eager beavers, wanting to know everything and hanging on to her every word.

"How are they? How are you? Are you in pain? What's the postnatal ward like?" Myself and Lynn threw question after question at Leanne before she even had time to respond to the first.

"Woah! One at a time" Leanne joked raising her hands in mock self-defence.

"The girls are doing really well but they will have a couple of weeks ahead of them in NICU as they need to gain some weight and learn to feed" she told us as he showed us multiple pictures of her beautiful girls.

"Wow, they are bigger than I expected!" I said feeling so proud of my new friend.

"Have you names yet?" Lynn asked.

"Yep" Leanne replied with a beaming smile. "We had always decided on the name Ellie for one of them but we didn't have a second name" she continued.

"After meeting the girls', we felt Robin was a fitting name for the other one as she was "robbing" all the placenta!" Leanne giggled.

"Oh my god, that is hilarious" myself and Lynn said in unison as we howled laughing.

I can't remember the last time I properly laughed and it felt good. Soon it was time for Leanne to go back and be with her girls, promising to come and see us again soon.

* * *

The next morning started as usual, after the usual breakfast and chats with Lynn, I popped down to the ultrasound room for my doppler scan. Mel was on again today and we had our usual daily chats as she started doing the scan, soon she went quiet intently focusing on the screen.

"It's not good today, is it?", I asked her.

"No, it's not," she replied, with a worried look on her face. "It looks as if the placenta function has really slowed down. When this happens there is a risk of it reversing, which would be very worrying." She didn't say much more than this and just got the consultant on call to come for a look.

When the consultant arrived and looked over everything, I just knew. This was it, today was going to be the day.

"You are going to deliver today, aren't you?" I asked.

"Yes, it's time," she said.

They told me to go back to my ward and ring Andrew and tell him to come in, she would meet me there and go over the plan. She stressed that although it would be happening today, this wasn't an emergency yet and we had a few hours.

"Try and stay calm," she said.

Calm. How could I stay calm? It had been ten days, TEN DAYS, since I was admitted to hospital with the hope of making it to 34 weeks gestation and now here I was at 30 weeks gestation and the babies would be born today. I rang Andrew and told him it was time, he needed to get here.

As I made my way back to my bed there were two midwives already waiting for me, obviously they'd already been made aware of the news.

"How are you feeling?" they asked.

I was still a bit numb at this point I think, I hadn't cried as I was trying to stay level-headed about it. I knew this day would come, just not this soon.

"I'm okay, but nervous," I shared.

"That's to be expected," one said. " The consultant will be up soon to talk through the plan and the anaesthesiologist from the theatre will come talk to you too."

I nodded, overwhelm and anxious worry setting in. "Please God, let everything be okay," I willed.

Andrew was in within half an hour and, as we saw each other, the emotions started to build but both of us danced around it trying not to be the first to cry.

"June Eleventh," the midwife said. "That's going to be your boys' birthday!"

We both looked at each other and all bets were off - we both started to cry. The poor midwife felt so bad, she was only trying to lighten the mood and instead she broke us like two kids who had just been refused a chocolate bar.

As the consultant arrived, she brought with her the anaesthesiologist and a paediatric NICU doctor who would take turns to explain to us how the procedure would go and what to expect after. We knew the boys would have to go to NICU, that was a given knowing they were being born 10 weeks early, but hearing the doctor speak about it brought it all home. This was going to be very different from my birth with Harry and I silently gave gratitude that I got to experience that with him as this time it would be oh so different and it was now time to board that rollercoaster.

Within two hours of being in the dark, quiet ultrasound room with Mel, I found myself being wheeled into an operating theatre with its lights so bright they were blinding and so many bodies in blue scrubs scurrying around I lost count. Andrew wasn't in the room yet; he wasn't allowed in until the surgery was about to start. I was scared, suddenly I realized I wasn't just giving birth to our boys but I was having surgery! Needles, I hated needles and there were much more than needles in this room. My shoulders started to shake as I convulsed into tears.

"I can't do this!" I cried as two nurses ran to my side trying to sit me back down on the bed I was now leaping from.

"It's normal to be scared but you've got this," they told me.

"Please don't leave me," I said to one of the nurses, as the anaesthesiologist was getting ready to give me the spinal block.

"I won't," she said. And she didn't, I was sat on the edge of the bed hunched over as she hunkered down in front of me cupping my hands, we locked eyes and chanted together over and over: "It's going to be ok".

Soon Andrew was in the room and the spinal block had kicked in as my legs just felt like a heavy extension of my body with no feeling. Two surgeons looked at us from the other side of a blue screen, "we are going to start now," one of them said.

Andrew held my hand as we waited in nervous anticipation to hear our boys' cries. Theo came first, we heard his tiny cry escape his tiny mouth, as I released a breath I didn't know I was holding. He was taken straight over to the incubator where he was assessed by the paediatric doctors.

Before we even had time to register it, Freddie was here. His cry was louder despite us knowing he was smaller. "He was mighty", I thought.

We got to give them both a kiss before they had to go to NICU. Their little bodies lost in the thick blue blanket and their faces barely evident under the pink and blue striped hats.

They were here. Our boys were here. Breathe, Tracy. Breathe.

After being stitched up and spending an hour in recovery as the spinal block wore off, I was brought to the postnatal ward. There, I lay on a bed in the tiny four-bed room, the air was heavy and hot. The high I felt after the boys were born was slowly starting to fade, like air seeping out of a balloon. I didn't belong here.

The other three mums were all sat cradling their newborn babies in that raw postpartum haze of overwhelm, pain and exhaustion, yet bursting with love for this little soul who's now made it safely earthside. Not me though, my babies were in the NICU and I didn't know when I would see them next.

The other mums were attempting breastfeeding, trying to establish that latch and having that all-important skin-on-skin, breathing in that perfect newborn smell that if you could bottle, you'd make millions. I, on the other hand, had a nurse standing to my left encouraging me to hand-express colostrum into a small purple syringe. I felt empty, my babies no longer inside me wriggling about, fighting for space. I had never craved anything more - I just wanted to hold my babies.

Just then Andrew returned after accompanying the twins on their journey from the theatre to the NICU unit.

"How are they?" I asked, jealous that he'd already spent longer with them than I had.

"The NICU consultant is going to come and speak to us in a few minutes," he said, without answering my question. That is normal I guessed. They needed to be in the NICU and I needed to be here, of course a consultant would come and speak to us, it was the least I would expect.

Andrew had brought me one of their little hats to have while I was separated from them. The little pink and blue stripped hat was stained a rusty-red from blood and at that moment it was my most treasured possession.

"Hi, Tracy. Hi, Andrew," the NICU consultant chirped as she entered the ward. "I wanted to update you both on your boys. They're doing well, and as to be expected they're getting a little support from the CPAP machine. CPAP stands for continuous positive airway pressure, so we're giving them all the air they need."

I felt a little relieved.

"Theo weighs 3.6lb, which is a great weight for 30 weeks. And Freddie weighs 2.5lbs, but we were expecting that, after the doppler scans," she continued, before pausing to gather her words.

"There is something I need to tell you though," she said as she perched herself on the end of my bed.

"Oh no," I thought, there is something here, of course there is something here. Consultants are very busy people, surely she doesn't have the time to check in with mums on postnatal wards, she's needed elsewhere.

Then came the six words that would irreversibly change my world forever.

"We believe Freddie has Down Syndrome."

I remember everything about that moment. The ringing in my ears so loud it felt deafening, my hands clutched so tight around the blood-stained hat that my knuckles were white, the blank look of shock on Andrew's face - one I had not seen before in our 11 years together.

I feel like we both held our breath for the longest time before either of us spoke. The silence was almost painful.

My instant reaction was to want to rewind those two minutes. It's funny how life can change in literally the blink of an eye. Two minutes ago, life was different, we had from being a family of three to a family of five. Yes, were born early and we had a tough few weeks ahea   a lot of twins are born early and are ok, surely, we would be the same.

"That is not possible," I said eventually, "you cannot have twins with only one of them having Down Syndrome."

"It is possible," the consultant said delicately. "It's about a one in a million chance, but it does happen."

She went on to tell us that over 50% of babies born with Down Syndrome have heart complications, so before coming to tell us this news they performed an echo, which is essentially a scan of the heart to check the structure and function of his heart. She told us his heart was perfect. I guess I should have been relieved but her words felt like they were flying over my head as they left her mouth.

I asked her if the issues Freddie was facing in pregnancy were because he had Down Syndrome. She said yes, that sometimes when babies have a different genetic makeup it can cause issues to arise but because we hadn't had any genetic testing done in early pregnancy there was no way of knowing this for sure. She said they would be doing a blood test to 100% confirm his diagnosis but those results wouldn't be back for a while.

"So, there is a chance he might not have it then," I asked, my voice raising a number of octaves in hope.

"Technically, yes, but I wouldn't be here telling you this if I wasn't sure myself," she said. She told us he had markers such as almond-shaped eyes, a flat nose-bridge and shorter limbs which would all be strong indicators.

She left soon after to let us process the news and said she

would see us in the NICU in a little while and would answer any questions we had. We sat together; I cried as Andrew comforted me. To anyone looking from the outside it would look like we were grieving and that our boys hadn't made it. In reality, we were.

We were grieving the life we thought we were going to have.

We were grieving the twins we thought we were going to have.

It hit me hard, so hard that it was stronger than any sleeping pill, as my eyes - heavy from tiredness and crying - slipped into sleep.

Chapter 3

Later that night, after the nurse shift-changeover, a midwife came to talk to me and asked if I planned to breastfeed. I felt like it was a pretty stupid question, I mean I did *plan* to, but my boys were currently in incubators in a neonatal unit, I hadn't 'planned' for that – hadn't that changed everything? Holding that frustration inside, I told her I would've liked to but I knew it wasn't possible right now. She seemed to ignore my words, instead telling me how beneficial my milk would be to my premature babies, how all babies benefit from their mothers' breastmilk but this was much more vital for babies whose immune systems are compromised. She told me she would give me a pump and to use it every 3 hours – even throughout the night – in order to bring in my milk and maintain its supply. I knew the request was obvious, from a health perspective, but inside I was screaming 'what about me?!' I've just had surgery, my babies are on CPAP in NICU, I've just received a postnatal diagnosis for one of my boys and now I need to pump around the clock while sitting in a room with other mums who are physically breast or bottle feeding their babies. It all felt relentless and just downright unfair. Where was the support for mums here? We matter too but somehow in that moment it felt like nobody cared about me – just my babies.

Of course, I didn't say any of that, I agreed I would do what she said and I meant it. Of course I would do whatever I needed for my boys but that didn't mean the thought of it wasn't exhausting.

"I'll be back in a moment with the pump," she said, turning to leave the ward.

"Wait, before you do," I said, pushing my internal dialogue aside. "Can I go to see my boys now? My husband is already down there. And I have full feeling back in my body, so I really want to see them."

"I'm not sure that's a good idea," she replied, trying to convince me otherwise. "You've had a major surgery and you need rest. Why don't you wait until the morning?"

"Please, bring me to my boys," I pleaded, I was done complying.

"Okay" she said, when my pleading wouldn't stop. "Let me source a wheelchair to bring you down. It's too far to walk only hours after surgery. I'll be back shortly."

* * *

As I was wheeled into NICU, I was taken aback by what I saw before me. Eight incubators sat in the dimly lit space, while the constant hum of machines cut through the deafening silence. Each incubator held a different baby, each with a different story of how they had found their way there, each with a parent worrying by their side. Each parent's face had pain, exhaustion and heartbreak written all over it, their hands slipped through the hole in the side of the incubator cradling the tiny hand inside. This is where I belong now, I thought.

It struck me that back in 2018, on that postnatal ward with Harry, I was one of those other mums I now shared a room with. I was sat cradling my newborn and learning to breastfeed and totally oblivious that only down the corridor this unit existed with these parents and babies inside. I immediately dreaded having to go back there, it seemed like some kind of cruel joke that I had to share that ward again with mums like 2018 me. How was that fair? This is where I needed to be and these were my people now.

Right at the end of the room stood two incubators side by side – Andrew sat between them.

"They are so beautiful," he said.

As I got up close to them, I gasped, I was shocked with how tiny they were – I mean teeny tiny!

I noted on their incubators it said "Luckie Twins born 3.01pm". Luckie was my maiden name and the irony wasn't lost on me right now.

They were both lying on their tummies with tiny CPAP masks on their face that were giving them breathing support. They needed this as they were so small and born so early and their lungs needed to catch up. The nurse assured me they wouldn't need them for long as they were both doing really well and holding their own.

Although there was only one pound in the difference, you could really see that in the boys. Straight away I could tell who Theo was, he was bigger by a mile - or so it looked. I couldn't believe they were here; it was so surreal. They both had feeding tubes coming out of their noses. I was told they would have these for at least 4 weeks and ideally, they would get mostly – if not all – breastmilk through it.

"Go easy on yourself," the nurse said, "It is hard enough to bring milk in and supply solely for one baby never mind two, so do what you can and we will supplement with formula where needed."

I felt my shoulders drop a little, finally someone understood. I guess my best is all I can do and my best will have to be good enough.

As I shifted my gaze between the boys, my stomach flipped. I was more drawn to Theo and when my gaze would rest on Freddie, I felt a feeling I can't explain. Was it fear? Resentment? Rejection, maybe? Whatever it was I tried to ignore it, hoping it would pass.

As I slipped a shaky hand in each incubator, the tears of a silent cry rolled down my cheeks. Their skin so warm as I felt the gentle rise and fall of their breath.

"I'm sorry," I whispered.

"Why are you sorry?!" Andrew demanded.

"I'm sorry I couldn't keep them safe for longer, I am sorry we are here," I confessed.

"This is not your fault, Tracy. You know that, right?" Andrew asked, without getting a reply.

I knew he meant it but I couldn't help but blame myself. Had I done something to make this happen? One in a million chance of having the kind of twins we do, why us? It seemed so unfair. My thoughts went to Harry, God, I missed him. In that moment I felt like I wanted to run, to escape this place and cocoon myself at home with him, I wanted to feel his head on my shoulder as he slept, I wanted to breathe in his smell – that smell meant 'motherhood' to me. The smell of this room felt clinical and foreign.

* * *

A little while later I returned to my bed. As I pumped, I decided to do some research. "How can you have twins with one having Down Syndrome" I googled. I am ashamed to say I knew nothing about, or nobody with, Down Syndrome. I had an idea in my head that it was a severe disability and I did not know it took genetic testing in pregnancy to find this out - I assumed it would be picked up in scans. "Why did we never consider testing?" I thought. I wondered would it have made a difference; would we have still continued with the pregnancy had we known? I really couldn't be sure of that answer.

I went on to learn that Down Syndrome occurs when there is an extra copy of chromosome 21 present in a baby's genetic makeup. Typically, a child will have 46 chromosomes with 23 coming from the mothers' egg and 23 coming from the fathers' sperm. However, sometimes an extra copy of chromosome 21 can occur meaning those babies would be born with 47 chromosomes. The copy of the extra chromosome changes the way the baby's body and brain develop and the medical term for Down Syndrome is actually *Trisomy 21*. People with Trisomy 21 share a lot of the same physical features as the consultant told us earlier that afternoon. People born with Down Syndrome also have a form of an intellectual disability that can affect their speech and how they process information. All this new information made my head hurt but before I was about to stop looking, I read something that BLEW.MY.MIND.

The article I read was about twins and Down Syndrome. I was fascinated by the facts contained within it.

Twins occur in approximately 1 in every 65 pregnancies.

Down Syndrome occurs in approximately 1 in every 444 pregnancies.

Twins with one having Down Syndrome occurs in approximately 1 in every million pregnancies.

Twins with both having Down Syndrome occur in approximately 1 in every 14 million pregnancies.

Now for the really interesting part…

Of the 1 in 444 pregnancies carrying a baby with Down Syndrome, only 20% of those babies will survive the first cell division. Furthermore, only 20% of that 20% will survive to fertilization and of that 20% only a further 20% will survive to birth. When you add that to the chances of having a twin pregnancy and the chances of having twins with one having Down Syndrome, it was pretty incredible. If I wasn't feeling like I was drowning in despair that we now made up some of these statistics, you could say it was a miracle that Freddie had made it here. Maybe one day I will, I thought.

When I stopped reading, I rang my best friend, Nicola. Andrew had already told our parents but I wasn't strong enough to speak to them yet.

"CONGRATULATIONS!" she excitedly screeched down the phone. I immediately started crying.

"Oh my God, what's happened?" her tone now very soft and cautious.

"Freddie has Down Syndrome," I exclaimed through breaks in sobs. Nicola let me cry, doing her best to comfort me with her words but I think we both knew I just needed to cry and for someone I knew and felt safe with to hold that space for me. No judgment. And she did that.

"It is going to be ok; I am here for you and we will get through this," she cried with me as we ended our call.

The next few days went by in a haze, I was told I would have to stay in the hospital for four nights to recover from the c-section. Every morning I woke and would mentally scratch off one more night, it was awful. Being on the ward with all those new mums with their healthy babies was punishing. I felt alone and scared and had a deep ache in me to have the warmth of a baby on my chest.

I lay awake at night shedding silent tears, fearful for what the next few days would bring. At the same time, I could hear the mothers in the beds beside me coo at their little ones, as they hungrily gulped their milk. It was torture. Where they had connection, I became isolation. I would wake up every 3 hours, pump and then walk down to the NICU to deliver said milk.

I remember seeing another mum on those late and lonely walks to and from the NICU along the brightly lit postnatal ward corridor. We never spoke but the gentle nod of the head as we walked slowly past each other in our dressing gowns and slippers with the knee-high white compression socks visible covering our legs, a war-wound reminder of that c-section surgery we were now recovering from.

She got it.

Without speaking I knew she was feeling the pain I was feeling, I knew because I could see it in her eyes; her weary and puffy yet determined eyes. Damn, us mothers are strong. Despite our exhaustion and pain, we were still here, showing up and fighting the good fight and, despite the pain and hardship and all the uncertainties that lay behind the door or that neonatal unit, the one thing I was certain of was that we wouldn't stop trying to show up and fight the fight.

Seeing the boys kept me going. We were constantly being told how well they were doing and that they were making great strides. I was producing enough milk for them to both exclusively receive breastmilk but only just. It meant every time I pumped, they needed that milk - there were no reserves. I was told when I went home, which would be the following day, I would have to get at least one milk delivery to them during the night.

It was a lot of pressure on my shoulders but I knew it was of benefit to the boys, so we'd make it work. You could visit the NICU 24 hours a day if you wanted, they only asked for you to leave during shift-changeover twice a day and in the case of an emergency with any baby in the unit. Having said that, they encouraged you leave at night to get rest, rest was important.

I asked at what point do they decide a baby is ready to go home, they told me there were five main factors:

They needed to be off any breathing support;

They needed to be out of the incubator and in a cot;

They needed to be minimum 35 weeks gestation;

They needed to be minimum 5lb in weight; and

They needed to be feeding on their own without the tube – either breast or bottle.

"Okay, so we had minimum five weeks here," I said to Andrew, my impatience kicking into gear.

"Ok back up, let's just take it a day at a time. First step is getting the lids off those incubators," he calmly directed.

After four nights of torture, I was discharged from hospital and sent home without my boys. Since the moment they were taken from my body, I had felt this emptiness creeping into me. I felt like a failure and to be now sent home without them in tow felt unnatural and cruel.

My only saving grace was that I was going home to Harry. Thank God for Harry. When I saw him for the first time in what felt like months, I embraced him like I've never embraced anyone in my life. He was medicine, medicine for my broken mama soul. Harry, although only almost three, had a lot of questions about why I was home without the boys.

"Where are my brothers, mama?" Harry asked innocently.

"Well sweetheart, the boys came a little bit too early and they need to stay in the hospital for a few weeks until they get a bit bigger but I promise we will get them home as soon as we can" I replied trying to hold it together.

"Ok, mama. Can we go to the playground now?" His resilience amazed me. He seemed just so happy to have me back. I knew the feeling.

I put him to sleep in our bed that night and told Andrew I needed him close. Truth was we had only recently got Harry sleeping independently in his own bed a few months previous. We had co-slept for a long time, so I knew it was a risk bringing him back in. I was worried Andrew would think we were going backwards.

"I know we have worked hard to get Harry sleeping independently but I just need him close right now. Ok?" I pleaded.

"Tracy, you don't need to explain. I get it. Harry has been in this bed since the day you went into hospital. I needed him close too" Andrew whispered as he stroked Harry's sleeping face.

It made my heart hurt a little to hear Andrew admit that. I realized then I forgot about Andrew, he was hurting too and needed his comfort and reassurance as much as I did.

"We will get each other through this" I said as I hugged them both.

That night would set precedence for how our routine would go for the foreseeable. After being at the hospital for the day we would come home and after putting Harry to bed, we would eat and talk and I would then pump as we watched TV. Andrew would then head back to the hospital with milk and to give the boys a goodnight kiss. I would climb into bed with Harry, as I snuggled with him beside me, his head on my shoulder as I craved. I would drift off holding that little blue and pink hat that had become so invaluable to me. It was the only bit of my boys I had right now and it helped me feel close to them while I was so far away.

* * *

The next few days visiting the hospital were hard, there is no other word to describe it. I have heard the phrase "rollercoaster of emotions" so many times, I've even used it myself, but I didn't truly understand it or experience it until this time. When I would wake in the morning, for those few split seconds, I would forget what we were going through, but as soon as reality hit my belly would drop from the inside like that feeling you get when you hurl downwards after reaching the climax of a rollercoaster. I would feel that gut-wrenching anxiety take hold and immediately ring the hospital for an update on how the night went. It was always positive, thank God for small mercies. It wasn't long before the boys were taken off CPAP and that removed a lot of worry.

Once I got to the hospital each day, I immersed myself in being with the boys, I felt content just being with them. I would read to them and talk to them all the time; the nurses would always say how important this is for babies ongoing development. It seemed silly to me at the time, they didn't have a clue what was going on, but it made me feel useful and like I was doing something for the boys, so I continued.

There was a little boy in the incubator next to the boys. His parents would both be by his side all day long and we would speak a little during the day but not much. It is such an intense environment and you would feed off everyone's energy. I could tell that little boy was not doing well. Although doctors would be as discreet as possible when talking to parents, it was such a confined space that you couldn't help but overhear.

When the boys were just over a week old and I went to the hospital in the morning as planned. As soon as I walked into the boys' unit I could feel the energy, it was heavy. When I sat next to the boys one of the nurses came to talk to me, she asked that I leave in an hour as the family of one of the other babies needed the room. I knew what that meant and so I squeezed my boys' hands a little tighter that morning.

As I left NICU a while later I saw the parents of the little boy who was next to the twins enter the room with some friends and family and my heart broke. As I went to the pumping room to pump, I cried. LIFE CAN BE SO UNFAIR! That poor little beautiful boy. His poor parents. How do you say goodbye to your baby? It is just not natural for your children to go before you at any age but as a newborn, with the hopes and dreams of this new chapter, of this new life... It is just downright cruel.

Andrew arrived before we were allowed back into the room, so I told him what was going on. He let out an exaggerated sigh with his hands intertwined behind his head as he said, "I just want our boys out of here". I knew the feeling. This place felt like being inside a ticking timebomb, everything was uncertain and you just hope and pray you make it out as unscathed as possible.

From that day on, I carried more emotion than I knew how to handle. It felt like a backpack weighing me down. I was so sore from the surgery, the word c-section gets thrown around so much that you often don't realise the weight behind that word. It is abdominal surgery and in any other circumstance you would be put on strict rest to recover but not in the case of surgery to birth your baby. The show must go on and I was finding it tough to recover myself whist being so much to everyone else.

I was also struggling with breastfeeding. As the boys were getting bigger, they were needing more volume and gradually their need was outweighing what I was producing. The stress it was causing me was overwhelming, I felt like things were spiralling out of control and I didn't know how to reign it in. Freddie's diagnosis was also weighing heavily at the front of my mind, I was so focused on getting out of NICU and getting them home, but I struggled to comprehend what life looked like at home now we had a child with Down Syndrome.

The official news of Freddie's diagnosis came one morning recently when Andrew was on-shift with the boys. I will never forget the phone call he made to me; I was home with Harry playing in the garden when my phone rang and I immediately knew by Andrews more serious and formal tone than I was used to that he was about to relay some important information. "It's been confirmed Hun, he has Down Syndrome". I immediately burst into soft tears. "Hey, we knew this Tracy, this was just confirmation" Andrew said gently. "I know but I was still holding onto that glimmer and now I have to let that go" I whispered. Just then Harry came and sat on my lap so I ended the call with Andrew as I wiped away my tears and forced myself to put on the brave face for my boy despite the heaviness that was weighing on my heart.

As the heaviness soon became too much to handle, I relayed all of my concerns to a nurse and she told me she was going to have a medical social worker come talk to us. Immediately I froze. A social worker? Were my parenting skills being questioned, I wondered. Maybe I should have just kept my mouth shut. The nurse must have seen the wide-eyed surprise on my face because without prompt she said a medical social worker is a facility in the hospital to be the go-between from parents to doctors and can help break down information and generally just be a sounding board. They were solely there to support the parents and make this time a bit easier, so we agreed to meet with them.

* * *

"Tracy and Andrew?" said a blonde-haired woman in a shirt and trousers, and not the blue scrubs we were accustomed to seeing everywhere, as she approached us. "I'm Sinead, a medical social worker here at the hospital, it's lovely to meet you. "Would you like to come have a coffee with me?" She asked kindly.

We both nodded in unison as we squeezed our boys' hands before leaving.

"How are you both doing?" She asked as she handed us both a coffee in her office on the ground floor of the hospital, another area I was unaware existed.

"Not great, it's a lot right now" I replied honestly.

"I have dealt with so many parents that get a postnatal diagnosis and so I know how scary it must feel" she said. "I can't tell you how to feel or how long you will feel this way but I am here to help with any practical stuff like filling in any forms or for any information or support networks you might want or need. I will help lighten the load where I can so lean on me" she continued.

We poured our hearts out to Sinead and by the end of the conversation I knew she was going to be an integral part of getting me, of getting us, through this time and although I was so relieved to have that support now, Sinead was not the only one now in our corner. As my support system grew Leanne joined that group. We had gone from sharing antenatal space together to now sharing NICU space together. Our boys were not in the same room as Leanne's girls but we would meet each other in the pumping rooms or for a coffee break. I felt like there had been a shift in our friendship, I had thought we were sharing a unique experience together - both having twins only days apart but I suddenly felt like I didn't deserve to put myself in the same category as Leanne and her girls. My boys were different, it felt wrong to even call them twins. Leanne had been so lovely when I told her the news.

"Tracy, your boys are beautiful and are made of tough stuff.

Although life won't be as you pictured it will still be wonderful" she said kindly.

I wanted to believe her, but I didn't. Leanne's girls were doing so well and were getting ready to be transferred to a different hospital closer to where she lived outside Dublin. We promised to stay in touch and I knew we would.

Lynn had also been discharged as they felt she was in a safe enough space now to continue her pregnancy at home. I was so pleased for her but a part of me wished the three of us were still in that antenatal space together, oblivious for what was to come. Although it was only weeks ago it seemed like a much simpler time.

***

As the weeks passed, life became mundane. The relentlessness reared its head again. Wake, breakfast with Harry, send Harry to childminder, hospital, home, sleep, repeat – with a lot of pumping in between.

Numbing, relentlessness.

I would see Sinead every couple of days, some days for a quick chat, others for a sounding board. It was on one of these days that I completely let my guard down and said exactly what I was feeling, I couldn't hold it in any longer. The words that I couldn't bear to admit fell from my mouth. Feelings that I felt deep shame for even having come pouring out as she sat there patiently listening.

I didn't want Freddie.

I didn't know if I had the strength to do this.

I didn't know if I wanted to.

I didn't ask for this life.

I had been wondering if I had missed that scan at 28 weeks what would have happened?

Would Freddie have quietly slipped away without us knowing?

Would that have been for the best?

So. Many. Questions.

No. Answers.

I waited for her to look at me in horror; to say I was the worst mother who had walked the planet. But she didn't. She nodded and said that what I was feeling was normal, that I was in shock, that I didn't know what the future held and that was terrifying. Despite her understanding I still felt like a terrible person.

Later that night I did more googling: "twins, one with down syndrome". After scrolling for a while, I came across a blog post by a woman in the UK who had twin daughters – one with Down Syndrome. On the blog was her Instagram handle so I looked her up and scrolled through her page, they looked happy.

"Would we be happy some day?" I wondered.

I decided to message her and reach out. I sent her a private message explaining I had just had the boys and got a postnatal diagnosis for Freddie and it was a surprise. I didn't want to tell her what I told Sinead, as I felt that would be hugely offensive to her. She messaged me back within the hour and she was so compassionate with me. She told me her diagnosis was postnatal too and it came as shock, she said she was so upset and felt like she was grieving and questioned whether she wanted her daughter.

She got it. I wasn't alone.

I felt it was okay to open up about my feelings then and I did, she was so kind to me and I was so glad I reached out, she told me she was there anytime I wanted a chat and I knew she meant it. Before we left it there, she asked how the consultant broke the news. I told her she was positive about it and when I said Freddie would have no quality of life she disagreed. She told me I was lucky; her consultant broke the news to her and swiftly gave her an adoption leaflet in case she wanted to give her daughter with Down Syndrome up.

I was dumbfounded. What is wrong with some people?

* * *

We were about four weeks in at this point. The lids were off the incubators and we got to do something I had been longing for the longest time to do - dress the boys. When they were in the incubator, they didn't need clothes as the incubator regulated their temperature. I had got so used to seeing them in just a nappy. One of my immediate thoughts when we found out we were having two boys was that we would save a fortune of clothes as I had kept everything of Harrys. However, Harry's first baby grows wouldn't go near the boys, we needed to buy premature baby clothes. If you could see these babygrows you wouldn't believe it, they were unbelievably small. They looked like proper babies dressed now, it's funny the little things you take for granted. It is such a privilege to be able to do basic things for your child and I wouldn't forget that.

It was in this moment, with both boys dressed, that I told Andrew I was ready to share with our extended family and friends about the boys' birth. We hadn't told anyone apart from our closest friends, family and work about the boys' birth, I am sure word had got around but it wasn't something we had shared ourselves. I told Andrew I wasn't ready to share about Freddie's diagnosis yet but we would soon. With both boys perched on my chest I took a selfie and posted it to my Facebook and Instagram telling everyone they were here and nearly ready to come home. Congratulations flooded in and I immediately felt like a fraud. Would they still celebrate our boys if they knew one of them had Down Syndrome? Was that worth celebrating? I felt like I was being dishonest but, despite that feeling, I still wasn't ready to share.

We were almost there; we were only a few days off them being 35 weeks gestation. Theo was already 5lb and he was getting used to feeding from a bottle. I decided not to breastfeed, it was going to be too much pressure so I decided I would pump for as long as I could but I wouldn't physically breastfeed. There had been so much talk over the last few weeks about volumes of milk and how much they needed to grow. The volumes were meticulously calculated by a dietician and I felt that I needed to know at home how much they were physically taking to keep my anxiety at bay.

Freddie was a little bit behind; he hadn't reached the 5lb mark yet and he was struggling with his feeding and still needing most of his milk through the feeding tube. The doctor explained to me that individuals with Down Syndrome have something called *hypotonia*. Hypotonia is another word for low muscle tone, it means all the muscles in their body are a little "floppy" and they need physio as they get older to work on that muscle strength. This low muscle tone can also extend to the mouth and tongue and so would explain why Freddie was talking longer to grasp it.

I felt like it was the first glimpse into my future of having a child with additional needs and I wasn't sure I was up to the task.

As Theo checked off the five 'ready to leave' list, Freddie fell further behind, until it became obvious that we wouldn't be leaving with both boys at the same time. That broke my heart. I wanted out of this nightmare and setting our sights on leaving NICU seemed like the first step. I didn't know how much longer Freddie would need to be here and I just hoped that having to physically split myself between the boys wouldn't cause me too much overwhelm or send me into total melt down. I knew I was already on shaky ground.

* * *

A couple of days later, Theo's big day arrived. It was a humid Thursday in July, we walked into the neonatal unit knowing for the first time we would be leaving today with one of our babies. The boys were 35 weeks gestation and Theo was thriving and now comfortably drinking on his own. It was a beautiful moment seeing the tube removed from his nose and seeing his gorgeous face properly for the first time. He looked so like his big brother Harry. It had taken a few days to get our heads around the fact that the boys would be coming home separately. I don't know that you can ever prepare yourself to split up your babies and every time the thought would come to the forefront on my mind I would push down, not yet ready to face that reality head on.

As we strapped Theo in his car seat, the feeling was so bittersweet. On one hand, I was so happy and proud that Theo had overcome this hurdle and was now ready to come home and be nurtured in a natural environment but the thoughts of still having a baby in the NICU made my stomach flip. If I am being honest, I felt most sorry for myself.

We had been through so much in the last few weeks. Theo had been such a trooper; he didn't ask to be born early and was thriving in the womb but he came out and took the last few weeks in his stride without complication and we should now be allowed celebrate that. I had visions of the four of us cozied up on the sofa watching movies and settling into this new life but that wouldn't be happening. I still had to come here. I still had to show up for Freddie and leave Theo at home with family while I did that. Truth is, I didn't want to do it, I wanted to be at home with my newborn baby and I didn't want to step back into this unit ever again. However, I soon pulled myself together and knew that was a tomorrow problem and for today we got to pretend everything was ok and enjoy this moment. So, with stinging eyes and shaky hands, we left the neonatal unit.

We went home.

Chapter 4

"Mummy, Daddy, baby!" I heard Harry scream as we unbundled ourselves from the car.

"Harry, oh my gosh, are you ready to meet your little brother Theo?" I asked my excited toddler, who looked fit to burst.

"Yes! Yes! Yes!" he shrilled.

"Harry, this is your brother Theo. Say hello," Andrew encouraged.

"Hello Theo," he said, resting his head on Theo's lap, as he hugged him, car seat and all.

Watching Harry meet his little brother Theo for the first time was surreal. Until that point, it felt like we had been living two very separate lives – one where we had a family at home and another in that unit in a Dublin hospital. Watching those two worlds come together was a magical moment and one I couldn't have prepared myself for.

Harry was in awe of this tiny little human and watching him holding his little brother made him suddenly look twice his age; he now looked like my little boy and not the toddler he was to me only the day previous.

Despite soaking in this wonderful moment, it was still there, that tug on my heartstrings so fragile it could snap at any moment.

Freddie wasn't here and that lack of presence was felt but like I had done previous, like I was doing every day, I pushed it down. It felt like I was a pot of boiling water on low heat; the feelings were simmering away but I was not allowing it to come to boil, not today. This day was special and I wanted to remember it.

Our families came over later that day to meet Theo for the first time. No family members were allowed visit the boys in the neonatal unit, so for the last five weeks they had only seen their new grandson and nephew through video calls. Today was an emotional one. Watching tears fill their eyes, I knew they weren't all happy tears, some fell in grief over Freddie's absence. Looking at Theo in his moses basket while the one next to him laid empty was the elephant in the room nobody wanted to address. Really though, what could they say? There were no words and there was no rulebook to follow, it was just an awful situation.

Andrew having to go back to the hospital that night was hard. When I say he had to, that is how I felt; Andrew wanted to. You see, Andrew had come to terms with Freddie's diagnosis much sooner than I had. His view was that he is our boy, he is part of our family and yes, his developmental path will be different to Harry and Theos' but we would learn how to walk that road and everything will be ok. I don't know why I couldn't see things that way, I wished I could, I really did, but I didn't. I couldn't shake the feeling that I knew in pregnancy something was up. I was always well aware Theo was more active than Freddie and I had this gut feeling all the way through my pregnancy that I would be punished for not wanting twins and only wanting one baby. "Was this my punishment? Had I manifested this?" Those thoughts crippled me.

When Andrew left that night, I snuggled both my boys in bed and it felt glorious. This was the life I pictured, my two boys. "Just let yourself enjoy this for tonight, Tracy, deal with tomorrow when it comes," I told myself.

* * *

The next day we mapped out a plan for this next stage. We decided I would go to the hospital four days a week and Andrew would go three, and we would ask family to do the nightly milk run to the hospital. Andrew would have to work on the four days I was in the hospital meaning we had to rally family to mind Theo those days too. It also meant there was zero time for me, Andrew, Harry and Theo to spend together at home. Zero. That thought made me feel mixed emotions of anger and sadness. I felt like we were being robbed of this precious time together; time we wouldn't ever get back.

Our family were only delighted to help and, between the grandparents and my sister, they all took on designated days. I should have been grateful for the support but instead I wanted to scream from the top of my lungs "I DON'T WANT TO GO BACK THERE; I WANT TO BE HERE!" I felt like a child being back in school having to go to history class when I couldn't think of anything worse. Why was this happening? That was the resounding question that haunted me several times a day and I was always met with the empty note of silence.

The next day I went to see Freddie. Stepping into the clinical neonatal unit for the first time after bringing Theo home felt different. I had always felt the emotional pull between home and this unit when both boys were here and Harry was at home but the pull felt even stronger now. I struggled to weigh up who needed me more. Obviously as Freddie was in hospital, it seemed natural that his needs were greater but really, were they? He was only here as he was having feeding issues and couldn't come off the tube yet, he wasn't in a critical situation. Theo on the other hand was at home, he was still too early to be here at only 36 weeks gestation. How could I leave him, albeit with grandparents, he needed me! I was his home and he needed ME. But then I would see Freddie, all vulnerable and alone, and I knew he needed me too. I felt like I was in quicksand and I was sinking; slowly, oh so slowly, sinking.

As I sat with Freddie chatting away as I usually did, the nurse approached and asked did I want to give Freddie a bath with her. I hadn't bathed Freddie yet so I agreed. He was so small and light at only 4.5lb, he felt so fragile. As we bathed him together his little frame looked so lost in the portable green baby bath that wasn't big by any means. After we dressed him, I sat with him nestled into my chest. The feelings were still there, I still didn't feel the strong instinct of connection to Freddie that I did to Theo but when I stared into his big, beautiful almond-shaped eyes and I looked past the diagnosis I just saw this wonderful little boy who needed me as much as my other boys did and that thought terrified me. I knew that if I allowed myself to look past Freddie's diagnosis now and just see him as him, my boy, I wouldn't be able to walk out that door and go home. Maybe some disconnection was what I needed to get me through this.

Maybe I needed to feel like I didn't need Freddie for me to survive this time.

When he would come home, I would allow my guard to come down and maybe my feelings would grow; I thought. But right now, it's staying up; protecting me like a shield of armour. "He has Down Syndrome. He has a disability and this is not what you pictured, or wanted, for your life," I would go on to tell myself, hammering myself back to reality with a bang.

* * *

I was still continuing to pump every three hours and it was exhausting. Freddie was currently getting all breastmilk and Theo was getting half breastmilk and half formula, I wasn't producing enough milk to exclusively feed them both breastmilk anymore. The pumping was relentless and I knew that as the weeks went on, they would only need more and I wasn't willing to put that pressure on myself. I made peace with the fact that my breastfeeding journey would likely end soon, as I only had enough energy in me to get me so far and, if something had to give, it would have to be the pumping and I was okay with that.

For the next couple of weeks, we continued to live life in limbo. Every day felt like Groundhog Day and I began to feel a feeling I had never really felt before: resentment, such strong resentment. We were in the height of summer and other families would be having beach days or picnics in the park. I'd see neighbours and friends out living their lives while I felt like mine had been put on hold.

I even started to feel some resentment towards Andrew. For four days a week he got to escape this horrible version of reality and go to work, he got to use another side of his brain, that side of my brain had now been made redundant at this point. Truth was, I would never be able to focus on work now even if I tried;

my brain was foggy and only had capacity for so much. That thought made me sad though, I never thought in my wildest dreams that I would ever not care about my work. God, this had really done a number on me, I thought.

* * *

Soon 3 August arrived. It was Harrys' third birthday. I had been holding this date as a goal in my mind. I hoped we would have Freddie home so we could have a proper family celebration and I really believed we would. I could see it all so clearly in my mind; we would all be out the back garden sat round the large circular rattan table. Harry would be in his element in his new treehouse that we had got him as his gift and myself and Andrew would each have a twin on our knees as family fought for who got to hold them first. Despite how clear this vision was, it wasn't to be. Freddie was still struggling with the feeding. There were two more weeks to go before he was full term, their due date was 18 August, so the new goal was that he would be home by then; but my scepticism was growing by the day.

I rang the hospital as usual that morning for a check-in on how the night went, there was nothing new to report. I told the nurse we wouldn't be in today as it was Harry's birthday and we wanted to celebrate him. I told her one of us would be in that evening and my mum would be in before the party with some milk. It was the first day since they had been born that neither myself or Andrew went to the NICU during the day, my heart hurt so much knowing he would have nobody sitting beside him all day talking to him and giving him cuddles but I knew Harry deserved this day; I also knew how incredible the neonatal nurses were and they would give Freddie some extra love today.

We had such a lovely day, hearing Harry's joyful glees as he opened present after present and watching him devour his jungle-themed birthday cake was just the tonic we all needed. There is something so healing about the innocence of children at play, watching them take so much pleasure in the little things; we could all do with taking a leaf out of their books.

"I can't believe he is not even meant to be born yet" my mum Pam said as she cradled Theo in her arms.

"I know it's pretty surreal alright, it feels like he has always been here though" I replied as I stared in awe at my tiny newborn.

"Freddie will be home with us before you know it, love" Paul said sensing what we all weren't saying.

"Mwah!" right on cue Harry landed over on Theo planting a giant icing-coated kiss on his brothers' forehead. "Can Theo have some cake mummy?"

"Oh no love, he is still too little, he can only have his milk" I said as I attempted to wipe his mouth as he batted me away.

I worried during my pregnancy how I would have enough love in my heart for more children as it felt like my heart could explode as it was just with my love for Harry but I came to learn it's not as simple as that.

My experience of birthing again after Harry was not that my heart immediately needed to double in size straight away but more so that the love starts all over again. I couldn't love these two new babies as much as I did Harry, he has had three years of my love and my love grew for him as every day passed and every milestone he reached. My love soared on some days – the day he said mama for the first time or the day he took his first steps across our kitchen floor. Not forgetting the first time he proper belly laughed – it was at a duck quacking by the way! Thinking about experiencing those days all over again with Theo brought more much-needed hope to my wounded heart.

Another thing I fully believe is that the first-born child is born first for a reason. Harry was exactly what I needed to learn how to be a mama, he was the perfect teacher and my bond with him was unshakeable. I couldn't imagine not having him by my side as we were going through this traumatic spell in our lives. He was 100% made to be a big brother too, I just knew my two younger boys were going to be the richest boys alive having Harry as their big brother, their protector, their friend.

As I tucked Harry into bed that night, he cupped my face.

"You are the best mummy in the world," Harry whispered. "I had the bestest day of bestest days today."

Oh, my little love, I thought. Despite life being upside down and inside out right now, I had to remember to soak in the joy because there can always be joy right? And this moment right here; that was joy personified.

* * *

Over the next few days life resumed as it had been. It was on one of these days as I was in the hospital that the boys' consultant, the one who was on duty the day of their birth, asked to speak to me.

"I want to do more investigating as to why Freddie isn't grasping the feeding" she announced.

"One of the doctors said it's because of his hypotonia and that he will get there eventually?" I replied not sure if I was making a statement or asking a question.

"Yes, and I agree with that to an extent but we repeated Freddie's echo today, the ultrasound of the heart, and it does show that Freddie has something called *Pulmonary Hypertension*".

Oh, here we go. Déjà vu. More bad news.

"You told me his heart was perfect!" I exclaimed in panic.

"Structurally his heart is perfect, but the pulmonary hypertension didn't show up then and pulmonary hypertension isn't anything to do with the structure of the heart," she said.

She went on to tell me that pulmonary hypertension happens when the pressure in the blood vessels leading from the heart to the lungs is too high. She said it was mild at the moment and he didn't need any medication for it right now but it could be causing him to tire quicker when feeding so it would need to be kept an eye on by a cardiologist.

My head hurt from this new information. I didn't think I could deal with any more bad news; I really wasn't sure how much I had left in the tank to climb this uphill battle that seemed to have no summit.

"I am going to send in a referral to the children's hospital cardiology team and we can take it from there" the consultant continued.

I uttered an insincere thank you as I left the room and headed straight for Sinead's office. Really my first port of call should have been to call Andrew but right now I needed to offload.

"I'm sorry for arriving without an appointment but I really need to speak with you" I declared as Sinead answered the door.

"Of course, come in" she responded as she ushered me in. "What's going on?"

Sinead's office felt like a second home at this point, despite it still being quite a medicalized environment with its laminated healthcare prints on the walls and the large white medical bin sitting in the corner. Maybe it was because when I was in Sinead's presence it didn't matter where we were, she always wanted to talk about how I was doing first - not the twins, not Harry, me! She made me feel like I was important in all this too and I was grateful for that.

"Oh Sinead, when will it end? Apparently, Freddie has something called pulmonary hypertension now that is likely one of the reasons he is not feeding. They are putting a referral in to a cardiologist. I don't know what this means but I feel like I am drowning in bad news. When will it bloody end?" I cried in anger.

"I think it would be of benefit to you to speak to our psychologist here," she said delicately.

Usually, I would put up a fight, I always liked to think I didn't need help, I would battle on myself, but instead I agreed. I now knew I had reached a point where I was struggling to cope, I was struggling to see how the rest of the story – our lives – were going to unfold and that thought scared the living daylights out of me.

"I think I would like you to organize that please," I answered.

The following day I met with one of the hospitals psychologists Aoife Menton. I wasn't sure how much to divulge, I mean where did I start? Only 12 weeks ago my life was so different, I didn't think it was possible for life to do a complete 360 on you in such a short space of time.

What came out wasn't linear by any means, I jumped from twins to Down Syndrome to pulmonary hypertension to feeding tubes to pumping to Andrew to Harry to my lack of sleep to my lack of social life to my career that was now on the floor.

I don't think I came up for air once. Aoife listened and took it all in.

"Let's meet once a week, Tracy. I am here to support you" Aoife said.

My support system had now grown by one more.

After meeting Aoife and making a plan to see her weekly, either in person or on the phone, I felt lighter. Why had I struggled with my mental health for so long by not asking for help? I suppose the answer to that is the old age tale of mothers putting themselves at the bottom of the to-do lists, the kids must come first, right? But how can we put them first if we are not strong enough, or well enough, to be who they need us to be? The tug-o-war of emotions was all-consuming but I knew if I didn't start prioritising myself, even just a little, I was going to sink.

Over the next couple of weeks, things seemed to level out a bit. I knew I had to keep talking, there were so many emotions trapped in my body that sometimes it felt like I wasn't me anymore; I felt as if I was floating out of my body looking down on someone else. I had spent my whole life thinking I knew who I was; I was strong, independent and I didn't need help from anyone, but now here I was asking and taking help from wherever I could. It was survival. I would talk with Aoife and Sinead regularly and if I needed any emotional release, I allowed myself to go there but outside of this there was only one focus: getting Freddie home.

* * *

I hadn't told anyone about my feelings towards Freddie bar Aoife, Sinead and Andrew. This meant I had to pretend to everyone that I was desperate to get Freddie home. It was true, I did want Freddie home, but I guess my feeling around why I wanted him home weren't clear – not even to me.

The hospital made me uneasy, I was so triggered by the sounds, the alarms, the doctors running down the corridors when an emergency would alert or seeing a baby not make it. It was ALL triggering and I knew I didn't want to be in this environment anymore; it was draining the life out of me. I also knew I couldn't bond with Freddie this way; the doctors were still responsible for so much of his care, they dictated so much of how his days would go in NICU that sometimes I just felt like a spare part that wasn't wanted or needed. I didn't know what life held for us at home, or if my feelings would change, but I was certain that I would do my best to be the mum he deserves. He had fought so hard to be here; he deserved to be here.

Being in a heightened state of anxiousness all day in the hospital made me crave calm, my nervous system needed to regulate and, on those days, coming home and cuddling Theo did just that. I always needed him close after being in the hospital. On my days not in the hospital he would spend most of the day on me in the sling and in the evenings when I would come home to him after being in the hospital, we would fall asleep together. It wasn't just that I was craving being close to him; I held him close out of fear. Fear that he wouldn't know I was his mum. It is not natural for a mum to spend so much time away from her newborn baby, he needed me as much as I needed him.

"I'm your mama, baby boy," I would say to him over and over at night as I lay with him; stroking his striking blonde hair watching him fall into deep sleep.

When Theo came up in my next conversation with Aoife, I told her about my feelings and fears of not being with him as much as I should. Aoife told me about the *good enough parent*.

The good enough parent is a concept coined by an English paediatrician, Dr Winnicott in the 1950s who studied mothers and babies. Winnicott found that meeting a child's needs just 30% of the time is sufficient to create happy, well-attached children. Although I'm sure most parents would strive to do more than 30% it was comforting to know I wasn't failing Theo. With Harry, I had always strived to be the perfect parent and its bloody hard work trying to be perfect. Maybe I could now make peace that good enough parenting is enough – more than enough.

As the boys' due date, 18 August, arrived Freddie still hadn't made progress with the feeding so Andrew and I were called to meet with his consultant to talk about next steps. I knew what she was going to say, I hoped I was wrong but my fears were realized.

"We would like to get you trained up on NG feeding to send Freddie home with the feeding tube," she said. NG stood for nasogastric, it is a thin tube that is placed into the nose and passes down through the back of the mouth into the stomach and it's how people with feeding or swallowing difficulties get their food or medications into the stomach.

I immediately started the cry. I hated the sight of the tube; it made Freddie look sicker than he was and I knew it would draw attention to him – and us.

"I won't go out in public with him like that," I told Andrew, not being able to face the stares or questions.

"You can and you will," Andrew said with confidence.

Of course, we agreed, but the plan didn't stop there.

"I don't know how you will feel about this but I suggest we do the tube-feeding training here and then transfer Freddie to the children's hospital for a few days before going home- "

"What? Why?" I interrupted in surprise before she had a chance to finish.

"Freddie's ongoing feeding difficulties are not something the neonatal unit are equipped to deal with and so Freddie will need to undergo the supervision of a speech and language therapist to help him to feed. We could send you home and put in the referral to the children's hospital but we could be waiting up to nine months for an appointment and- "

"NINE MONTHS!" I interrupted again.

"If you let me finish? By doing the transfer and linking in with a therapist as an inpatient it will cut out that wait time. I know it's daunting but I think it's the best decision" she continued.

The thoughts of going to another hospital with more doctors and more sick babies made my chest feel heavy but the thought of having a baby at home with a feeding tube for nine months was a harder pill to swallow; so, we agreed to the transfer.

* * *

It was a couple of days later, Harry's first morning of pre-school, when my phone started to ring with "NICU" highlighting my screen. My heart sank.

"Hello" I answered breathlessly, fearing more bad news.

"Tracy, it's Emma". Emma was one of the NICU nurses. "Everything is ok. I am calling to let you know that we are moving Freddie this morning".

"What? No. Harry is starting school this morning. Can you transfer later? I have promised Harry I would be there and I don't want to miss it?" I begged.

"I am so sorry Tracy but the bed is available now in the other hospital, we need to take the opportunity. I will be escorting him don't worry" she assured me.

"Oh, thank you Emma, one of us will meet you there as soon as we bring Harry to school". Thank God for that.

We decided we would both take Harry to pre-school and then Andrew would dash off to meet Freddie at the children's hospital and I would follow in later that afternoon after collecting Harry from school.

As we stood outside Harry's pre-school, about to embark on this huge chapter in his little life, we did what we needed to do. We took photos and smiled; huge beaming smiles for the camera his grandparents stood holding. To anyone from the outside we looked like any other family of four; but we weren't. Instead, I was torn apart inside with conflict, knowing as those photos were being taken, our newborn son was in an ambulance driving across Dublin city without his parents by his side. I felt like an utter fraud but what else could I do? I was doing my best; that's all I kept reminding myself. This is a day I wanted to remember as a good day and so I battled through those feelings of conflict and knew we would face this next hurdle and soon we would all be together. Just a few more days and it'll be over, I told myself.

* * *

Later that day, after spending the afternoon with Harry and Theo and getting the low-down from a very excited and happy three-year-old on how his first day of school went, I entered the children's hospital and made my way to Freddie's room. It felt different here, good different or bad different I wasn't sure. Maybe it was because it was a proper hospital and not a neonatal unit. The corridors were brightly lit with murals painted on the walls; a large fish tank with lots of different coloured goldfish sat in the middle of the hallway with children gathered around it.

Freddie had his own room at the end of the corridor, there was a door leading to a back garden in his room, I wasn't used to seeing daylight or having access to fresh air in the NICU. He looked so tiny in the huge cot that sat centre-stage in the room with Andrew sitting in a chair beside him.

"Hi mum, I am Paula, Freddie's nurse today" a super friendly petite nurse in blue scrubs said as she approached me.

"Hi Paula, I am Tracy. How's he doing?" I asked.

"Oh, he is great. I was just chatting to Andrew there and I was saying I have read through his file so I know why he is here. Hopefully he will see speech and language tomorrow. In the meantime, I need you to bring in a few things - nappies, wipes and some clothes" she announced matter-of-factly.

"Oh sorry" I said confused "We have spent weeks in NICU and they provided everything, we weren't allowed bring anything in for health and safety reasons" I answered defensively.

"Yes, it's a little different here, mum" she smiled as she squeezed my shoulder. "Also, which one of you will be staying tonight?"

"Huh? Staying?" I asked as myself and Andrew looked from each other back to Paula.

We had not stayed a night with Freddie before; the NICU encouraged you to go home and rest, but here wasn't like that. It was starting to make sense to me that here we were Freddie's primary caregivers and not the nurses; we were expected to feed, change and look after him and we were expected to stay at night too. My initial reaction to this was fear; how would we begin to try look after three children with one of them not under our roof?

"I will be staying" Andrew responded eventually.

"It's only going to be a few days; we will get through it" he said to me as Paula left the room.

He was right, we knew Freddie was only here to link in with the speech and language service to get a plan on the feeding, then we would go home.

* * *

The next day, I went in to take over shift as Andrew went to work. I met with the speech and language therapist, or SLT as they were referred to, who told me the plan. She said she would observe him feeding over the next few days so she could assess where we are at and give us a plan to work on at home. We would also have a dietician who would work closely with SLT to ensure his needs were being met from a weight and growth gain point of view. It seemed straight forward but the impatience in me just wanted to have this done with now and be on our way but she said it would be about five days here.

My body tensed as I felt how hard it would be to do this; to physically split ourselves day - and now night.

As I sat with Freddie that afternoon, he was so peaceful asleep on my chest. It was then that I decided now was the moment we needed to share about Freddie's Down Syndrome diagnosis with our extended family and friends. I wasn't sure when this bout of strength would come again so I went for it. After consulting with Andrew, I took a picture of us together and wrote a caption about Freddie's diagnosis and posted it online. I knew I was writing words that made me sound more optimistic and happier than I was but I had hoped by putting it out there like that I might receive optimism and happiness back; and that I did. People were so kind and had such beautiful things to say about Freddie and us as a family that it gave me a glimmer of hope that maybe my own words would ring true to me soon.

Over the course of the next few days, we had a few sessions with the SLT and dietician and what Freddie's NICU consultant had said was correct; due to his prematurity and the hypotonia that comes with having Down Syndrome meant that he was still working on gaining the muscle strength in the mouth to suck and swallow. They were confident that with regular practice he would get there but they couldn't give an exact time frame. It also depended on how the pulmonary hypertension played out too, if that worsened it could affect the feeding so we would be seeing a cardiologist every three months. The SLT and dietician agreed to see us every four weeks but we would have phone consultations every few days so the volume could be adjusted if required. For now, we were only trying with 30ml of milk in a bottle at every feed and giving the remaining amount through the nasal tube. I was terrified about going home with a baby on a feeding tube, I knew I wasn't strong enough to face anybody's questions.

The next day it was time to bring Freddie home, it was 4 September. The beginning of September always felt like more of a new year to me than 1 January did, so it felt fitting to bring Freddie home as this new month began. Maybe this was the start of a new, more positive journey for us all, I hoped.

"Let's put this behind us and go home," Andrew said, as he took my hand. In the other hand, he held Freddie in the car seat as we walked through the long corridor and went home.

Chapter 5

Walking through the front door with Freddie in my arms, nervous anticipation flooded my body as we prepared to introduce him to our family. Harry and Theo were there with my mum, my sister Niamh, my brother Danny, and his partner and kids, and Andrew's parents.

My mum had already met Freddie a few days previous, the room we were in at the hospital had a door that led to a garden and on the other side of this garden was the car park. My mum met Freddie through steel bars separating the garden to the carpark; if it wasn't so messed up and emotional it would've nearly been funny.

My mum was so emotional meeting Freddie, she was his biggest cheerleader from the moment she found out he had Down Syndrome and would always speak about his diagnosis with pride which I was always so grateful for. Meeting Freddie meant more to her than anyone; she works as a special needs educator in a school working with children who have Autism so she is a champion in advocating for neurodiverse children and I knew how lucky we were going to be to have her expertise, patience and love on this journey.

The rest of the family hadn't met Freddie yet, so watching as they all gathered around him, tears rolling down their faces as they drank him in, filled me with emotion so raw it physically hurt. It had been 14 weeks, 14 weeks since he had been born, and nobody had met him yet; that thought blew my mind. We were a very close family on both sides, so knowing they hadn't met this little human who took up such a big place in our family seemed unnatural; but we were here now and that's all that mattered.

My heart broke every time I looked at Freddie and saw the long white tube coming out of his nose and taped onto his cheek. The tape caused a harsh redness to his soft and sensitive newborn skin. "I really hope he won't have it for long," I told the family before they even had time to ask. "Of course, he won't," they all replied in unison; the force in their voices was overly evident.

I knew we were all on the same page, we all had hope in our hearts that this was the start of a more positive journey than the last 14 weeks had offered us. They say it takes a village to raise a baby and our village were pretty incredible. We had been so lucky with the level of support, love, and compassion they had shown us these last three months. I had taken for granted just how much they'd had to sacrifice themselves in order to be here for us and I knew we would still need to lean on them over the coming weeks. They had all taken Freddie's diagnosis in their stride too; I don't know how I expected them to react but we were only met with positivity and optimism and I was so thankful for that and hoped it might rub off on me soon.

Just as he was besotted when he met Theo, Harry had the same welcome when he met Freddie. He showered him in hugs and kisses.

"I missed you, brother," he would say over and over. God, he made me so proud.

"What is that in his nose, mummy?" he asked.

"It's how he gets his milk, honey," I told him.

I explained that Freddie was not able to suck his bottles yet so he needed a tube to get the milk into his tummy so he wouldn't be hungry. Harry accepted this information without question and once again I was in awe of his resilience.

That night as my three boys slept, Andrew and I sat down to a take-away dinner and for the first time I felt calm. For the first time in 14 weeks, neither of us needed to be anywhere.

We were home.

"It feels good to be out of the hospital, doesn't it?" Andrew said.

"It does but I wish it was all behind us, we still need to get Freddie off the tube and educate ourselves about Down Syndrome now," I worried aloud.

"I know, but let's just enjoy this moment and take each day as it comes," Andrew replied.

As I got into bed that night, I decided to leave Andrew to co-sleep with the other two boys and I took Freddie into the spare room to co-sleep with me. I knew I needed to try to fill the emotional distance I felt between us.

As I pumped, Freddie slept next to me and I was suddenly so aware of his smell; that clinical hospital smell that I had become so accustomed to over the last number of weeks. I made a mental note to bathe him in the morning, I didn't want that smell to make itself at home here; we were past that now.

The feeding was still a real challenge but I had pulled back pumping during the nighttime now and instead I was doing three-hourly during the day but nothing from midnight until 6am. It meant I woke in agony with painfully full breasts in the morning but Theo had dropped his 3am feed himself so sleep was more of a priority than pumping at this point. I didn't know how that might change with Freddie home now; if he was up I might as well pump but we would see how it goes.

* * *

The next morning myself and Freddie lay in as we had been up a couple of times during the night. I was soon abruptly woken to Freddie's screeching cry; one I had not heard before. I swiftly turned to him to see what had caused the sudden emotion and something was different - the tube was out! "Shit!" I exclaimed! When I had rolled over, I had tugged on his tube which led it to come out and the tape had been pulled from his cheek. I could see by the red raw flush of his cheek that this had been what caused his outburst. I took him downstairs where Andrew was with Beth and Theo; Harry had gone to pre-school.

"I've pulled his bloody tube out," I cried in panic.

"It's okay we've been trained in this, stay calm and we will sort it," Andrew calmly replied.

Andrew went to retrieve the new tube and tape and said he would put it in. I held Freddie as Andrew fed the tube through his nose and down his throat; Freddie roared in response. He hated when the tube would be changed; anybody would, I guess. I mean getting a tube pushed from your nose down to your stomach couldn't be comfortable. I remember asking a nurse about it before and she said some of them had done it to themselves to experience what it felt like and she said it was like having a string of spaghetti down your throat – that is hardly pleasant, I thought.

After we finished, I caught a glimpse of Beth who was crying.

"Are you ok?" I asked.

"It's just so unfair. Unfair on Freddie, and you both, that you have to do this," she cried softly.

I felt equal parts sadness and frustration at her words. Sadness that this situation, our new life situation, was making her upset but also frustration that it had to be said. I mean what choice did we have? We had to do it whether we liked it or not.

"It's done now, at least we've got the first time out of the way," Andrew encouraged, his ability to always look at the positives present.

The next couple of days were chaotic, as we learned to navigate this new life of being a family of five with a preschooler and two newborns. It was on one of these days that we decided to take the boys out on a walk. I was so nervous; it was always a picture I held in my mind that I was fearful of doing. Would people apologize to us for Freddie's diagnosis or feeding tube? If they do, how will I handle that?

"You won't know until we do it so let's go," Andrew said as he bundled the boys into the double buggy, ready at the door for its maiden voyage.

It was a perfect crisp Autumn morning; the sun was shining but there was a slight nip in the air as the first leaves started to fall from the trees. As we took a stroll around the neighbourhood, we were met by two people we knew; I could feel my chest get heavy as they approached, waiting in nervous anticipation for what was to come.

"Congratulations!" they said as they looked at the boys wrapped up in the grey furry snowsuits and asked how we were doing; there was no mention of Freddie's diagnosis or his tube. I didn't know whether to feel relieved or offended. Both maybe? Even though I was scared of people asking me about the tube at least that would be an acknowledgement of what we've been through. Of what he has been through.

"You see, that wasn't so bad," Andrew said as we walked away.

"I want to go home," I told Andrew. I wasn't ready to do this, my chest was feeling heavier and tears were stinging the corner of my eyes. It was just too much, too soon.

As we went home, I cried.

"Why can't we just have normal twins? Why do we have to change tubes or learn about Down Syndrome or go back to the hospital for heart scans and feeding appointments? What have we done to deserve this?" I sobbed to Andrew.

"Look Tracy, this is our life now, we didn't ask for this but it's what we've been given so we just need to get on with it," he said, sounding exacerbated.

"What if I don't want it! Where is my choice in all this? What about me?! Why don't I matter?" I roared back.

It was our first fight, our first fight since the boys had been born, and it had been simmering for a while. I was always thankful Andrew was so level-headed and positive; it was the trait I loved most about him but sometimes I just wanted to feel like I wasn't alone in my feelings and that sometimes life could be shit and I didn't have to try to see the positive side… All. The. Time.

I was well aware and educated about matrescence at this point, I knew the birth of a baby, or babies, also signified the birth of a mother but I was really starting to feel like us mothers, the mothers who are struggling, are the forgotten ones. We are tired, we are depleted, we are navigating a new chapter and it matters. We matter.

I didn't say this to Andrew though; I didn't have the energy for a deep and meaningful right now so instead I cried and he held me.

He held me as I cried, until I was exhausted and empty.

* * *

My mum came the next morning to help me, as Andrew had gone back to work after having the last few days off.

"Does Freddie's breathing look funny to you," I asked Mum. He seemed to be sucking in under his ribcage as he took breaths and the breaths seemed slower than normal too.

"He doesn't look distressed," she said. She was right he didn't look distressed but I had seen Freddie for weeks on end in a hospital incubator and cot bare-chested and I had never seen breathing like this.

"It's not right, I am going to bring him in to be checked out," I told her. She agreed to watch the kids as I called Andrew and we drove back into the same children's hospital we had only left four days previous.

As we got there, we went to A&E, it was really busy and due to covid restrictions they were only letting one parent in.

"You go home, I will stay," Andrew told me.

As I left and drove the 40 minutes home in autopilot mode, I couldn't help but think this was always going to happen. I could always feel in my gut it wasn't natural to bring a baby home on a feeding tube; for your life to suddenly become so medicalized. I was once again met with the feelings that I had brought this on myself; I was still struggling to accept Freddie and his diagnosis and feeding struggles so maybe this was what I deserved for not accepting my child – just as he was.

Andrew had a long night in the hospital; Freddie was struggling with his breathing as I suspected and his blood oxygen saturation levels were low, so he was put on oxygen. Although I was worried about Freddie, and Andrew spending all night awake in a hospital A&E, I selfishly felt a wave of calm in the home that I hadn't felt since Freddie had come home. I wasn't so on edge waiting to do the next tube-feed or anticipating having to run a new tube through his nose. The little things I took for granted with Harry when he was a baby now seemed like such a privilege – being able to breastfeed him to sleep, being able to co-sleep without fear of pulling out a tube and feeling content in that newborn baby bubble. Feeling safe, that's what I was missing, and feeling safe is such a privilege we take for granted.

The next morning Andrew called and said Freddie's swab results had come back and he had developed a cold which was affecting his lungs and breathing and so he would need to stay a few days in hospital until he was better and off oxygen.

"Can you come in and take over for a few hours, I've been up all night and I need a few hours' sleep," Andrew asked. I agreed, a knot immediately forming deep in my belly at the thoughts of walking that long corridor again.

"I'll ask your mum to come watch the boys and then I will be in," I replied.

After Beth arrived, I pumped and then hit the road into the hospital. As I drove down the motorway, I felt rage start to engulf my body, it was rising thick and fast like a volcano about to erupt and then it came. I screamed so loud I made my own ears ring. I was driving faster than I should have been, with big fat tears falling from my eyes as I let out scream, after scream, after scream.

I wanted it all to end; I couldn't take feeling like this anymore and I needed something, something to take this pain and god-awful suffering that ached my heart every moment of every day away. Was this rock-bottom? Do I really want to die? The dark thoughts took over my mind as I continued to drive, not knowing what to do next.

I wanted to not feel for a while, just not feel anything. I wanted to numb myself out, blank out the feelings.

"Just calm down and breathe," I told myself aloud over and over as I slowed my driving and approached the hospital.

As I parked my car, I realized I had driven to the wrong hospital, I hadn't come to the children's hospital Freddie was now in but instead I had arrived at the maternity hospital.

"You absolute idiot!" I screamed at myself. As I went to get back in my car, I stopped. Suddenly, I felt this inner voice saying, "This is where I need to be".

I turned on my heel and walked straight through the reception of the hospital, through the double doors and arrived in front of the large heavy-wooden brown door. I pushed the intercom and was met with the familiar voice of the receptionist.

"How can I help you?" she said cheerily.

"Sinead please," I replied.

As the door buzzed open, I walked the few steps towards Sinead's door and knocked lightly, a knock that didn't match the heaviness in my body. As Sinead opened the door, a look of surprise washed over her face as she took in my red-raw tear-stained face.

"Tracy, what's wrong," she said. I didn't respond, instead I fell. I fell to my knees on the unwelcoming harsh carpet floor and with my face in my hands I sobbed so uncontrollably my whole body shook with convulsions.

"Tracy, what's happened? Is it Freddie? Is he ok?" she asked.

"He is back in hospital on oxygen," I told her in-between sobbing gasps.

"Ok just try to breathe and we can talk about this, you are safe here," she said gently.

Safety. That's all I wanted right now, but it was so far out of my grasp.

As I calmed down, I found myself in the chair opposite Sinead with both my shaky hands clasped around a plastic cup of water.

"I noticed yesterday Freddie was breathing funny so we took him to hospital; he has a cold and is on oxygen and will be there a few days," I told Sinead.

"I am sure that was scary but well done for spotting the signs something was wrong," she said.

"I am meant to be there now, I am meant to be taking over from Andrew; he's been up all night but I can't go there, I just can't!" I exclaimed; the tears coming again like another rolling contraction.

"Okay, let me ring Andrew and tell him you are here," she said. As Sinead went to call Andrew, I felt so guilty. Andrew had taken on so much of the burden when it came to Freddie's hospital admission, he was trying to keep our business going without my support, trying to be a present dad to our boys at home and visiting Freddie in any spare moment in-between. He needed me to step up and be strong, he needed me to be an equal participant in this absolute shitshow but I had hit a wall. I had nothing left in the tank.

"Andrew is on his way here," Sinead said.

"What?!" I said, the panic evident in my voice.

"He can't leave Freddie alone, Freddie needs him!" I cried.

"You need him more right now, Freddie has the nurses looking after him, he's in safe hands".

I tried to tell Sinead that the children's hospital was different, parents took a much more active role in their child's care there but I knew she was right. I was in no fit state to do anything right now.

"I don't think I want to be here anymore," I told Sinead as I sobbed. "I don't want to leave my boys but I just can't do this anymore, I can't take any more," I continued.

"Okay, I am going to get Aoife to come speak with us, is that ok?" Sinead said knowing this conversation had now gone down a path we had never been on before. I nodded in agreement.

As it turned out, Aoife wasn't in that week so Sinead said another therapist would see me in a couple of hours.

"Are you happy to see him," Sinead said. I nodded again in agreement, although a bit nervous at it being a "him", but I was in no position to refuse right now.

As Sinead and I talked more, she said something that surprised me. "We'll see what the doctor says but I think you need rest and maybe you need to go to hospital to get that," she said.

"I don't want to go to the hospital," I told her.

"It is completely your choice but I think it could benefit you to get some rest" she said. I sat with the thought but didn't respond.

Andrew arrived a lot quicker than I expected, he must have bolted as soon as he hung up the phone. As I saw him walk through the door, the look on his face mirrored what I was feeling inside; he looked scared, unsure of how bad I must be to have landed here. He knew me, he knew I always had my shit together. Even in the last few weeks, when we were going through such a stressful time managing all our kids' care while keeping the business afloat; I was always organized, I always had a plan. Not now though, I was all out of ideas and I think he knew that.

"Why didn't you call me?" Andrew asked.

"I didn't know I was coming here," I explained. "I just drove and found myself here. I can't go there, Andrew, I'm sorry, I know I'm letting everyone down but I just can't be there. I have no energy left." I cried.

"Shhh, it's ok," he said gently as he hugged me tightly. "How are we here?" I thought.

A little while later I found myself up on the fourth floor of the hospital. I was in the office with Dr Anthony McCarthy, a perinatal psychiatrist in the hospital.

"Tell me what's going on," he said kindly. I told him everything from the boys' birth to the last few weeks to now.

"I have nothing left to give, I am exhausted and don't want to feel this way anymore," I cried again.

"I have twins," he said, "they are grown up now but when they were born, that first year, its survival. So, to be going through what you are is tough, very tough, and we are here to help you."

"Sinead said maybe I need to go to hospital, what do you think?" I asked.

"It is your choice; I agree you need rest but I don't know if you need hospital," I knew by saying hospital we were talking about a mental health hospital here. I had said I no longer wanted to be here; I knew how serious of a statement that was.

"I think we should put you on some medication to help with your anxiety and some sleeping pills to help you to get some good sleep," he said.

"I can't take sleeping pills; I have kids to look after and I have to go to Freddie," I said surprised at his recommendation.

"You need to mind yourself, Tracy," he said. "You need rest and sleep. You are no good to anyone if you are not okay; are there people at home who can help you? Some sleep will really benefit you."

"Yes," I mumbled, the emotion building making my voice tremble knowing how hard it would be to ask for even more help from our families who were already doing so much. Why wasn't I stronger? I used to be so strong, I didn't recognize myself right now. As he wrote a script, he agreed to keep in touch.

"I will call you tomorrow and every few days after but get rest at home and ask for help to do that," he said. I agreed I would, not sure how honest I was being by doing so.

* * *

As Andrew and I got into the car, we took a moment before leaving. "Were you crying?" I asked Andrew, his red-rimmed eyes were all the answer I needed.

"Yes, I spoke with Sinead while you were upstairs. I wish you told me how hard you were finding this," he said, his voice cracking.

"I didn't know until today how bad it was, it's like I snapped today and it's surprised me too," I replied.

We went to the pharmacy on the way home, as I took out the two packets of pills, I felt nervous about the thought of taking them, I had never taken medication bar the odd paracetamol for a headache and the thoughts of taking medication that would maybe knock me out or change my mood scared me.

"I don't know if I want to take these. I know the doctor said this will help and he was really kind and supportive but I am afraid of not being awake. What if I miss something?" I said to Andrew.

"I am not sure if medication is the answer either," he said. He was scared of what I would become on these meds and I got that, I did too but what was the alternative? "Maybe we should go to one of the hospitals," Andrew said.

"No!" I cried. "Those places are for people who have real metal health problems, I don't belong there!" I exclaimed.

"You are struggling, Tracy, it might help?" he responded.

"Let's go home," I sighed as we drove home.

* * *

As we walked through the front door my shoulders felt heavy as if all my responsibilities were physically waiting at the door for me and I had to load them on as I walked through. Playing with Harry, feeding Theo, pumping, making dinner, bathing the boys – the thoughts exhausted me.

"Theo needs his bottle; do you want to give it to him?" Beth asked me.

I swear to God, she might as well have asked me if I wanted to run a marathon because the weight I felt at the thought of sitting with my baby giving him his bottle felt the same as the thought of doing one. What is wrong with me?

"Would you mind? I have to go upstairs for something," I responded. As Beth started to give Theo his bottle, Andrew followed me upstairs.

As I walked into my bedroom, I sat on the floor and sighed so heavily I felt my whole body physically exhale in response.

"Why are you sitting on the floor?" Andrew asked, as the worry spread across his face.

There was a bed and a chair on offer, I could have had my choice, but it was the floor that called me. My body needed to feel the ground right now.

"I don't know," I shrugged, wondering how to tell my husband just how broken I felt.

Before my thoughts could gather themselves, I began to cry.

"I just can't do any of this anymore, Andrew," I sobbed, keeping my eyes on the floor, as Andrew sat down next to me. "I am just too exhausted; physically and mentally. My heart breaks every time I walk into that ward and see Freddie there. I'm failing on all fronts. I can't even give Theo a bottle for crying out loud! I don't have any energy left to be the mother I want to be. It's just all too much."

"We need to get that second opinion," he whispered, wrapping his arms around me.

The thought of going to *that* hospital – a mental health hospital – terrified me. All sorts of thoughts intruded my mind and I couldn't stop them.

"Would they think I'm a terrible mother?"
"Would they think I'm an unfit mother?"
"Would they try to take my kids from me?"
"Would they admit me against my will?"

Truth is, I didn't know what to expect and never in my wildest dreams did I think I would be considering visiting such a place; yet here we were.

As the thoughts continued to race through my mind like a bullet train, I felt my breathing rising and rising until I was struggling to catch up with its pace. My hands started to tingle and my head felt dizzy. I could hear Andrew talking to me but I wasn't taking in his words. I was so focused on catching my breath that I couldn't focus on anything except the white double-doors of the wardrobe in front of me. I inspected every part of it like it was the first time I had seen it. I was focusing, I needed to focus.

"Tracy, answer me!" Andrew demanded, the panic in his voice snapping me back.

"I think I just had a panic attack," I whispered.

I had never had a panic attack before so I'm not quite sure how I knew at that moment that it was one.

"Jesus, I thought you were going to pass out," Andrew sighed, before a strength took him. "Right! We are going to the hospital. Now!"

I didn't disagree; instead, I picked myself up off the floor, walked down the stairs and into the passenger seat of my car; not even acknowledging Beth or my boys as I did so.

* * *

The hospital was only 10 minutes from our house, which was a blessing really, there wasn't enough time to change my mind. As we pulled up to the large silver gates Andrew got out and pressed an intercom. He spoke for a couple of minutes into the intercom; I am not sure what he was saying, I couldn't hear. I wondered if he was saying his wife was going fucking insane, because that didn't feel too far from the truth.

As he walked back towards the car the large gates started to slowly open forward.

"What do I even say," I asked Andrew.

"Just tell the truth of how you are feeling," he replied.

As he pulled the car to a stop, I took in the surroundings; a large red brick building stood in front of us on green land that stretched for meters around it. It was quiet; peaceful.

As soon as we entered the building, we were greeted by a receptionist, who took my name and told us to take a seat, that a nurse would be with us shortly. It wasn't so peaceful inside, I could hear shouting coming from a distressed woman down the corridor, the sound terrified me. "Did I really belong here?" I thought wanting to bolt back out the door and through the gates.

"Tracy Holmes," a male voice called.

Too Late.

* * *

The room was cold, cold in temperature and in atmosphere. It felt clinical with its bare white walls and green plastic chairs. A large brown table separated myself and a male psychiatric nurse who sat in front of me.

"Tell me why you are here," he asked kindly. Jesus, where did I start. I told him about the boys' birth, Freddie's diagnosis and now Freddie being back in hospital.

"I am really struggling to cope," I said honestly. "Everyone keeps telling me how great I am and how strong I am, but I am not; I'm drowning." I cried.

"The psychiatrist in the maternity hospital has given me medications to take and although the thought of something helping me seems wonderful right now, I am also scared of not feeling anything," I continued.

"That makes sense," he said. "What are you scared about not feeling?"

"I am scared about not feeling the same about my boys because I love them; they are my world. I am scared I won't feel like me anymore and that I will lose a part of who I am," I said with more confidence than I felt.

After we talked a while longer, he said he felt like I didn't need to be admitted here and that if I felt I could try get some rest without the medication to try that and revisit it.

"I know it might be hard to imagine but maybe don't go to the hospital to your son, take some time at home with your other kids and relax too," he prescribed.

The thought of not going to the children's hospital upset and lifted me in equal measure. I couldn't imagine how I could not go there; what would people think of me?

As we drove home, I told Andrew about everything I had discussed with the nurse. Before I had left, we also agreed I would be linked in with a community mental health nurse who would check in on me in-person or on the phone as a support to me for as long as I needed. The thoughts of linking in with another mental health professional exhausted me, I mean how much more of my feelings and emotions could I really share? But it was support and I knew I needed that by the bucket-load right now.

When we got home, we asked my mum and Andrew's parents to be there. I told them I was having a hard time and was struggling and that I needed to take a break at home. I didn't divulge that I had had suicidal thoughts earlier that day or that we had just been to a mental-health hospital; I didn't want to worry them as I knew we needed them so much right now. We asked if they would spend some time at the hospital with Freddie if the hospital would allow it, allowing me to be home with the other boys. They all agreed without hesitation; once again I was so humbled and grateful for them willing to put their own lives on hold to support us; it can't be easy for them.

* * *

I struggle to put into words what the next few days felt like; a rollercoaster of emotions doesn't seem like it even touches the surface. I stayed home with the boys and didn't go to the hospital; for the first time since the boys were born, I felt like a mum again. I found my love for spending time and doing things for my kids again. I mean don't get me wrong being a mum-of-two is exhausting, there is never a minute but it was a completely different kind of exhaustion to what I had been experiencing the last few weeks.

I had also made another huge decision and that was to stop breastfeeding. It was extremely hard to come to this decision and I sobbed my heart out as I pumped for the very last time the night I got home from the mental-health hospital. They say never give up breastfeeding on a bad day but I knew, deep in my gut, that this was the right decision for me – good or bad day. I needed to realize I couldn't do it all and as beneficial as breastfeeding is, sometimes you have to put yourself first and if it's not right anymore then you know. And I knew.

Freddie wasn't getting any better over the few days, the cold was still there and his oxygen requirements were not decreasing like they hoped they would. Despite this, I still couldn't go to the hospital, how bad does that make me? Thankfully the hospital did allow grandparents to visit under the circumstances. Knowing they could be there when Andrew couldn't made me feel more at ease; but still I knew I wasn't winning any "mother of the year" awards!

I worried for Freddie, of course I did, but I had never experienced the feelings I had felt in the last week and I was fearful of my mind and the stories I was telling myself.

So, as I sat in the in-between of my two co-existing worlds; home and the hospital, with my mental health on the floor; I clung onto hope. Hope that I would make it out the other side.

Chapter 6

It had been a week, a week since I had seen my 4-month-old son. The guilt I felt was indescribable. I missed Freddie terribly, but as I spent each day with my two other boys a shift happened. For the first time in a long time, I felt like I was being a good mum.

I would drop Harry to pre-school and then walk or snuggle at home with Theo. I got so much peace by just being with him, he was such a content baby and reminded me so much of Harry when he was a newborn. I wondered how similar they would be as they grew up and if Theo would be as sensitive and kind natured as his big brother, I also wondered how having a sibling with a disability would affect them both.

"Would they have to stick up for him and protect him at school?"

"Would Freddie even be able to go to school with them?"

"Would Theo be bullied for having a twin that was *different* to him?"

"Would it cause us all to miss out on doing family adventures that Freddie might not be able to do?"

"Would they see Freddie as a burden on them?"

"What if something happened to me and Andrew, how would they care for Freddie?"

As I sat with these thoughts, cradling my beautiful little boy, tears slipped from my eyes onto his green jungle-themed onesie. "I'm sorry," I whispered sadly. And I was, I was so very sorry for what I had *done* to our family.

* * *

After a week, I decided I needed to go back to hospital. It felt like being in a job and I had just had a week of much-needed annual leave. Although things were busy at home, with the boys and general life admin, I did manage to get plenty of rest thanks to help from my mum, sister and Andrew's parents. They had all been incredible, they would spend time with Freddie in hospital and then come spend time with us at home, so I could get some rest. I felt guilty but so very grateful.

I had also made the decision not to take the medication, I wanted to see if the physical break from the hospital and the rest for my mind and body would help first. It did, it really did.

I had also been linked in with the community mental-health nurse called Kate. She had come out to the house to meet me and chat. We had a pleasant enough conversation and although she was there to support me, I felt like I already had enough around me at the moment. Aoife was continuing to call me weekly and I had built up such a solid relationship with her; I trusted her wholeheartedly and I felt like I could tell her anything – without judgement. Between that and my family, I felt like another "therapy" offering was too much. So, I told Kate I would call on her if needed but I felt supported enough right now.

As I walked into the hospital the next morning, my stomach was doing somersaults. I hated this place and I was resentful we needed to be here. Freddie was now up on the cardiac unit on the third floor. The virus that he had was affecting his pulmonary hypertension, which meant doctors needed to keep a closer eye on him from a cardiac point of view and this was obviously the best place for him.

This ward was different to the rest of the hospital. Everything was new and the rooms were big and spacious with a bed for parents to sleep in. It had big windows over-looking Dublin city letting lots of natural light into the room; something I was thankful for after weeks spent in the dark neonatal unit in the maternity hospital.

As I set my eyes of Freddie, I immediately starting crying – hard. He looked so tiny and vulnerable with his feeding tube and oxygen nasal probe making his little face hard to see in its entirety. I was such a shitty mother; how could I not be here for him when he needed me? I knew I was in an impossible situation, having to PHYSICALLY separate myself between my newborn twins - it's the most unnatural thing in the world - but that realistic fact means nothing when you are looking at your baby who you've not seen for a week.

Emotions took over and I felt the invisible line between us that had been there since he was born pull me closer to him. As I picked him up and nestled him to my chest, I felt a wave of protection I had not felt before and I was scared. He was my boy, as much my boy as my other two at home, and that feeling I had been waiting to hit me finally did. I love him – extra chromosome and all - and that was scary as hell. How am I ever going to be able to leave him now? Shit.

A short while later, a doctor entered the room.

"I am Dr Nesson, I am Freddie's paediatrician," she said.

"Hi," I mumbled, feeling embarrassed. "What must she think of me?" I thought. "I am sorry I've not been here; I was having a really hard time," I continued, no longer embarrassed to hide the fact I was struggling.

"You don't need to apologize, this is a really hard situation, go easy on yourself," she said, kindly placing a hand on my shoulder. I was relieved by her kindness.

"Fill me in then?" I asked.

"So, Freddie has rhinovirus, it's another word for the common cold. Sometimes with babies so young and vulnerable it can hit them harder and cause them to need hospital treatment, as it has done Freddie."

"Will he come off oxygen soon?" I asked.

"We have tried to wean him but he is still not ready to come off it, but we'll keep trying," she explained.

After the doctor left, I was having some quiet time with Freddie, when a cleaner came in and asked if she could give the room a once-over. I was sat in the corner on the large red recliner chair with Freddie asleep on my chest.

"I had a girl just like your boy," she said in a thick Dublin accent as she manoeuvred her mop around the floor in a zig-zag pattern with her eyes on the floor.

"With Down Syndrome?" I asked curiously raising my gaze from Freddie to her.

"Yeah," she responded.

"I was devastated when she was born and I was told she had it, I was so young and terrified, but she was the best thing to happen to me," she continued as she stopped mopping and faced me head on.

"How is she now?" I asked cautiously, already aware she had referenced the past tense a couple of times now.

"She died a few years ago, she was in her twenties. She had a heart condition; she was lucky to live as long as she did."

"I am so sorry" I said softly but genuinely as we locked eyes for the first time properly during our encounter.

"Thank you, love. Treasure that boy, he is a blessing," she smiled as she left the room.

"Everyone is rooting for you, aren't they buddy," I said to Freddie as he wiggled around my chest finding his comfort. "I promise I will do everything I can for you, I might struggle at times, but I will always try my best," I said as I stroked his soft downy hair.

I knew in that moment there was a shift, a shift in me that filled me with hope that we might be okay. It struck me that in all the conversations I had in the last few weeks with professionals, - Aoife, Sinead, Dr McCarthy, the psychiatric nurse in the mental-health hospital and Kate, it was a two-minute exchange with a cleaner in a small hospital room that opened my eyes wider than they had been since the day of their birth in June. Sometimes a mother's perspective, a mother who knows just how you are feeling, a mother who has experienced loss, a mother who is living with a broken heart; she is the only one who truly sees you and can lift you from that hole and guide you forward. And I had experienced that today.

I felt seen and understood for the first time since Freddie's diagnosis.

* * *

The next couple of weeks went by in a blur. We were back to our usual routine of balancing hospital and home and it was hard, extremely hard, but we were making it work. It felt different than it had during the summer; I think the fact that I'd stopped breastfeeding, I was fully recovered from the c-section and just generally being further post-partum meant having less hormones rushing through my body and that was helping me be a bit-more level-headed about our situation.

On one of my mornings at home, I was getting Harry ready for pre-school, when I noticed Theo was very sleepy. He had only been awake an hour, there was no way he could be tired, I thought. As I picked him up, I saw that his breathing was slower than normal and he was sucking in under his ribcage more than usual too.

"No! This can't be happening," I cried inwardly.

Just then Harry's childminder Niamh arrived, she was bringing him to pre-school.

"Niamh, there is something wrong with Theo, I need to call an ambulance," I said panickily.

"Okay, stay calm," she said.

I didn't want Harry to hear and get upset so I asked Niamh to leave with him but call into my friend Salley a few doors down and ask her to come up; Salley was a nurse so I knew she would know what to do. I rang the ambulance while I waited for Salley, although she was up with me in two minutes.

Salley had only had her second baby two weeks previous, I felt so guilty dragging her here but my mind was racing going to all the wrong places. Salley took Theo from my arms as I was pacing the room and told me to sit and calm down, she spoke to the paramedics on the phone giving all the medical lingo I couldn't take in; thank God she was here, I thought.

"He is going to be ok," Salley said.

"I can't go through anymore, why is this happening," I cried.

"Just go pack a bag, I will wait with Theo and we will see what paramedics say," she said calmly. I did what she told me.

The paramedics arrived within 20 minutes and checked his vitals right away; his blood oxygen levels were low. It was happening again.

"No Tracy, there is no time to feel sorry for yourself, pull yourself together," I told myself before I crumbled. And I did. I went in the ambulance with Theo as I rang Andrew to tell him what was going on.

"What do you mean you are on your way here with Theo?" he said surprised. Andrew was in the hospital with Freddie today and things were fine when I was talking to him earlier this morning, so he was understandably very taken aback. I briefly told Andrew what was going on and said I would call him when we arrived.

I had never been in an ambulance before and it wasn't an experience I had ever wanted to have either. We raced down the motorway, dodging rush-hour morning traffic as weaved in and out of lanes with the lights flashing and the alarm-sound deafening. Once we arrived, Theo was brought straight into the triage and assessed by the doctors, he had already been placed on oxygen in the ambulance. How could it be that I had spent my whole life well and had raised a three-year-old without a health complication and yet I had witnessed both my newborn babies being rushed to hospital and placed on oxygen within weeks of each other? As that thought sank deeper through my body, I started to feel my breath grow heavy and my body tremble as I started to shake and anxiously catch my breath.

"Are you ok?" one of the doctors asked. I shook my head unable to speak as I started to gasp for air.

"She's having a panic attack," I heard one of them say as she rushed to my side.

"Just breathe, breathe, breathe," she said as she clasped my hands. The feeling of her hands on mine grounded me as I started to catch my breath and focused on her words.

"Come outside with me for some air," she said when I had caught my breath and stopped shaking.

"Theo will be okay, we think he has RSV, which is a respiratory illness that can make it harder for babies to breathe when they have it but you did the right thing bringing him here, he will be okay," she said.

"You don't understand," I replied exasperated. "I have Theo's twin brother upstairs on the third floor in the cardiac unit, he has been in hospital since he was born except for 4 days at home. I am living my life split between here and home and I also have a three-year-old. It is out right exhausting and I cannot deal with Theo being here now too, it's too much," I cried.

"Wow, I did not know that and I am so sorry to hear that. You are an incredibly strong mother to be handling all of that, have you support?" she said.

"You know what?" I replied. "I have just about had it up to here of people telling me how strong I am. Trust me I don't want this life; I question every day what the hell I must have done in a previous life to deserve this awful situation I am in but what choice do I have? Is it okay if I am not strong and I run away from all of this? Will I be called weak and a terrible mother if I do that? Because that's what I want to do! I am not strong; I am just trying my best every day to keep my head above water but this – I said as my hands flew to the air in the direction of the hospital door – this is TOO MUCH," I shouted as I turned on my heel back into the hospital.

The nurse tried to get me to go for a coffee and take a breather but I needed to be with Theo. You see at this point I had made peace with the fact that maybe Freddie didn't know I was his mum yet. That sounds really sad but it's reality; he had a team of nurses looking after him on rotation every day since he was born and, since he had been in the children's hospital, we weren't staying every night either liked we would have wanted to; it was physically impossible with the kids at home and work. Any one of the nurses could be a mother's touch to Freddie, but not Theo. He had been home almost three months at this point and he knew I was his mama; I was his home and he knew it – we both did.

"We have a bed for Theo," the doctor said. "He's needs are not cardiac related but the nurse told us about your situation and we are so sorry for all you are going through so we have got Theo a bed up on the same ward as Freddie, hopefully that might make things a little easier for you," he said.

I started to cry; it was an incredibly kind gesture but all I took from that was that Theo would be staying in hospital.

"So, he's not going home then?" I asked.

"No, he needs to be here but hopefully it will only be a few days. RSV tends to peak days three to five, so it's likely he will get a bit worse over the coming days but he will then get better and go home."

"Worse? Christ!" I thought.

***

A little while later we found ourselves walking through the corridor of the cardiac ward that, a week out from Halloween, was currently adorned in cobwebs and skeleton decorations. Theo was put in room nine, only six doors away from his twin in room three. It was like being back in the NICU, only worse as they were separated this time.

"How is he?" Andrew asked as he entered the room, rushing to Theo's side and placing a kiss on his head.

"He has RSV and will be here a few days they think," I told him. Andrew rolled his hands through his hair as he let out an exaggerated breath.

"It's a lot, isn't it?" I whispered.

"Yeah," he replied his voice shaking with emotion. I knew then that I couldn't tell Andrew about my panic attack downstairs, I could tell he was on a knife-edge and I didn't want to push him over, so instead I put on a front as best I could.

"It's going to be ok; we'll get through this like we always have," I told him.

A nurse came in and interrupted us.

"It's best you two don't mix between rooms if you can help it, we don't want Freddie catching RSV," she said. I laughed in response. If I didn't laugh, I not only would've cried, I would've lost my mind.

"Makes sense," I simply said, my voice straight as a die.

The next few days were tough; the toughest part was being away from Harry and wondering what this latest development was doing to his little mind.

"How is he?" I asked my mum who was staying with him.
"He's fine, he's being spoiled rotten and being kept occupied," she said.

My mum and Andrew's parents were rotating his care while we stayed with the boys. "At least he's with family, so many people are not lucky enough to have family support the way we do," Andrew said. He was right, I knew he was right but it was still so hard being away from my little boy, I missed him so so much.

* * *

The doctor was spot on about the virus. Theo got worse on day three and it was hard seeing him so unwell. He was off his milk and needed a lot of suctioning, which he hated; the fear on his face as they pinned his hands down while they stuck a thin tube up his nose to extract secretions was heartbreaking. I would have refused it, except for the fact that it brought him relief. But he improved and I have never been more relieved to see it.

After six days in hospital Theo was allowed to go home. And with that came the moment I was dreading. I left Theo's room and had to walk past Freddie room to get out of the ward. It still wasn't advised that we mix them, Freddie was too vulnerable and Theo wasn't 100% better. I wouldn't have forgiven myself had something happened because of my own selfish need of wanting to see them together again. So, we stopped at his door and we waved. I could see the nurses looking, I could see the pity they felt for us all over the faces. I didn't want pity, I just wanted my boys home - together. So, we kept walking with tears rolling down my cheeks as we went outside to meet

Grandad Paul who was collecting us.

Once we got home something felt different. Suddenly my secure safe place that I called home no longer seemed so safe. I had been so focused on Freddie's ill health that I didn't stop to think how I would cope if something happened to one of my other kids. Maybe that was a good thing though; I didn't need another reason not to sleep at night. Thankfully, Theo was well now and I had to hold onto that but being in hospital with a sick child opens your eyes to a world you never knew existed, a world that holds a level of worry and anxiety that you never knew possible to feel and now that I had felt it I could never un-feel it. I was tainted by this experience now; my innocence had long left the building and I knew I would be hardened by this experience forever.

* * *

As the next couple of weeks passed, Andrew and I questioned how much longer Freddie would be in hospital. It had been nearly 6 weeks at this stage and he still couldn't come off oxygen and seemed to catch bug after bug. The poor kid wasn't getting a break but we knew there had to be more to it.

"We need to ask the doctors for a meeting," I said to Andrew, "I am going to ask to speak to the social worker and see if she can arrange it."

We had a new medical social worker called June in the children's hospital. We no longer had contact with Sinead since we were discharged from there, so Freddie's paediatrician linked us in here. The next day I spoke to her and she agreed it was wise at this point to call an MDT meeting, which stood for multi-disciplinary team meeting. At that point, Freddie was under the care of three teams: respiratory for his lungs because he couldn't come off oxygen; cardiology for his pulmonary hypertension; and general paediatrics for his general medical day-to-day needs. He also had a dietician and speech and language therapist for his tube-feeding and we had recently been introduced to a physio and occupational therapist who were doing a little bit of work each week on his physical development and strength. It was A LOT to keep up with and we felt like we were on a merry-go-round as there continued to be no talk about discharge from hospital.

The following day we met with Freddie's doctors from his three medical teams for their collective opinions.

"Freddie's swabs are virus-free at present but he's still needing oxygen, so we need to look further into that," said Dr Nesson, his paediatrician.

"Yes, we are going to do a CT scan now that Freddie's chest is clear, that will show us if there is anything else going on with his lungs. We'll also do a sleep study one night to assess his blood oxygen levels in depth while he is sleeping; children with Down Syndrome can be more prone to getting sleep apnea so this will look into that," explained Dr Kenan, one of the respiratory consultants in the hospital.

"And we'll repeat the echo to see how his pulmonary hypertension is doing – again now that he is virus-free," his cardiologist Dr Sugden shared.

I had a headache from all the information; I was so thankful notes were being taken, there was no way I would have remembered everything, but I was glad a plan was being formed.

Over the next few days all the tests were completed. The hardest was the CT scan; something that seemed so basic and straight forward actually wasn't for Freddie. As he was only a baby and they needed him really calm and still for the test, he needed to have a general anaesthetic. Nothing can prepare you for watching your baby be put to sleep; I was allowed to stay with Freddie until he fell asleep but then I had to leave. I waited out in the corridor with a constant stream of tears rolling down my cheeks as I pictured my little boy in the next room with a team of doctors around him. You can't fully understand the weight of the word "trust" until you have to hand over your baby in circumstances like this.

"Please let him be ok," I willed.

When Freddie came round, he looked even more vulnerable, I cuddled him harder than I had before. "I am sorry you have to go through this," I whispered in his ear.

We were back in his room when Dr Kenan and Dr Sugden came to see us. "We have some news," they said. My stomach flipped; I knew it wasn't good.

"Freddie's hypertension has got worse," Dr Sugden revealed. "It's not severe but its moderate and we would like to put him on medication for it at this point. He also has a very small hole in the heart; I am not concerned about it and would imagine it would close up in its own in time but seeing as he is requiring oxygen its worth closing it up to see if it helps."

"Open heart surgery?" I exclaimed in fear; knowing a lot of kids with Down Syndrome need open heart surgery for heart repairs.

"No, no, it will be by a procedure called a cardiac catheter; it's nothing like open heart surgery," he assured.

"From a respiratory perspective we have found some

worrying imagery from his CT scan," Dr Kenan interrupted. "A lot of kids with Down Syndrome will have some cysts around their lungs which Freddie has but he also has some other abnormalities we don't see a lot of."

"What does this mean?" I asked, panicked.

"There is no way to know exactly what the abnormalities are without doing a lung biopsy but that is far too risky and we wouldn't do that," he said.

"What will you do then?" Andrew interjected.

"In our experience lung abnormalities – or lung disease as we would call it – will improve with time as his lungs mature and he gets bigger and stronger but he may need oxygen for a number of months until it improves," he replied.

"Months!" I exclaimed, "We can't stay here for months?!" I cried.

"You wouldn't stay here, we would send you home with oxygen, other kids have gone home on oxygen," he said. The thought made my stomach fall from under me.

Oxygen. At home. Hell, no! I thought.

"This is a lot to take in," Andrew said. "It is," Dr Kenan said, "but there is more. Freddie does also have sleep apnea so he will need CPAP at nighttime when he sleeps." We went on to learn that sleep apnea is when your breathing stops and starts while you sleep and CPAP is a non-invasive ventilation machine that pumps air through the nose or nose and mouth to help with those non-breathing episodes.

We sat there in shock.

* * *

As the next few days passed, Freddie got set up on his CPAP machine. We were assigned a CPAP nurse called Mae, who was so caring and kind and from the moment I met her I knew we would get on. She explained everything about how the machine would work and set-up a plan to do training with us. It was all extremely daunting but I tried to keep my game-face on as, quite frankly, I was sick of feeling like the world was against me; it was exhausting and at this point it felt easier to just try and block out my emotions.

I was glad I was in that frame of mind when it came to the day of the cardiac catheter procedure, it meant another general anaesthetic and watching Freddie be put to sleep again. The wait is painful, watching the clock and trying not to imagine the worst that can happen. Knowing you're not in control of your baby's care needs is the worst feeling, I felt so helpless. Thankfully the procedure didn't take very long and we were back in his room within an hour and a half.

"How did it go?" I asked Dr Sugden eagerly as he entered the room.

"Really well," he said. "It was very straight forward but it will take a few days to see if the closure will help his breathing issues so let's wait and see."

* * *

A few days later we weren't seeing any improvements in his oxygen requirements, so we knew the closure hadn't done what we hoped.

"The closure hasn't sorted the breathing issues, has it," I asked Dr Sugden on his morning rounds.

"No, but I did tell you I didn't think it would," he said.

"So, what's the plan now?" I asked.

"We'll keep Freddie on his medication for his pulmonary hypertension but aside from that it's in the hands of respiratory now and from a cardiac point of view I'll only need to see him every three months to begin with," he replied.

It was bittersweet really; on one hand I was relieved his care needs were being downgraded slightly but I was also scared and nervous now that I knew a procedure wasn't going to *fix this* and we had to wait and see how his lung disease would play out.

The following day another respiratory consultant came to see us along with Mae; there were four respiratory consultants in the hospital and they rotated ward rounds every week. This week it was Dr Carmine; we had met her before and I really liked her, she had an approach that balanced both empathy and straight-talking facts and that was an approach I was on board with. Both Andrew and I were in today and I was soon glad of that for what she was about to say.

"Freddie isn't going to come off oxygen anytime soon, so we need to come up with a plan to get him home to you on oxygen," she said.

"How challenging is that?" Andrew asked.

"Look, it's not going to be easy, especially with other kids at home, but it will be easier than coming back and forth from here every day; I am sure you will agree?" she replied.

We both nodded in unison. I think she could see the fear on my face because I didn't need to ask anything before she spoke again.

"It's going to take a few weeks so this is not something you need to prepare yourselves for straight away; we will organize home-oxygen, training and make sure you are totally comfortable before leaving," she said.

"Ok well let's get the ball rolling then," I said, sounding more hopeful than I felt.

After she left, Mae stayed behind. "Are you both ok?" she asked kindly.

"This is going to be really hard and I am not sure we can cope with it," I said softly.

"We will get through this; it won't be forever," Andrew said.

"It's not easy but other families have done it and you will too; we are all here to support you," Mae said, as she gave me a much-needed hug.

Later that day myself and Andrew went to get a coffee. "They can't just send us home with a child on tube-feeding, CPAP, and oxygen; there has to be some help out there; I am going to speak to June about it," Andrew said.

I was relieved he felt this way, usually in our relationship Andrew was the laid-back one who took everything in his stride and I was the dramatic over-thinker, so I knew this was a big deal if he was feeling the pressure too.

The next day we spoke to her and she agreed there was help out there and said she was going to reach out to The Jack and Jill Foundation, who provided families with respite care for children with medical complexities. I had heard of the charity before but never in my wildest dreams thought it would be something we would need but right now we would take all the help we could get.

* * *

The next few weeks were a haze of meetings with doctors, home-oxygen training, CPAP training and meetings with a Jack and Jill coordinator who had kindly agreed to provide us with 32 respite hours a month. It all seemed so regimental and despite the awful reasoning behind needing all these meetings, my organized brain liked the planning and co-ordination business of it all; it made me feel useful again. However, the wind would soon be knocked out of our sails when days before a planned discharge Freddie caught yet another virus. This time it was the winter vomiting bug – norovirus -along with rhinovirus again.

"Christ, give the kid a break," I cried to Andrew on the phone as the swab results came back. Watching Freddie vomit continuously and be placed on fluids to hydrate him was heartbreaking; I never wanted to swap places with anyone more before.

"I wish it could be me instead of you, baby," I said to Freddie, as I held his hand.

A while later Dr Nesson entered the room. "I am really not happy with how he's looking and his oxygen saturation and gases are not good so we are going to move him to ICU," she said.

"ICU! What? What are gases?" I asked breathlessly.

"Gases are blood tests we do to see what a person's oxygen; carbon dioxide and PH balance are and Freddie's are really not good right now," she replied.

I struggled to take in what she was saying.

"Go and ring Andrew and tell him to come in then meet us in ICU, it's on the first floor," she said hastily. Before I even had a chance to respond, a swarm of doctors and nurses were in the room preparing to wheel him to ICU.

"ICU is for critical situations, is he going to die?" I cried.

"He is going to the right place, Tracy," Dr Nesson assured me.

As I ran outside, every part of my body was trembling so much that I struggled to navigate my phone to call Andrew, I had the sudden urge to vomit. I have never felt fear enter my body as quickly as it did in that moment, in fact I don't think I have ever felt fear like this before. Period.

"Freddie is going to ICU, get in here now," I said to Andrew.

"What? When? How?" Andrew asked in panic.

"I can't talk, I'm gonna be sick, just come now," I said.

As I hung up the phone, I ran to the nearest corner and vomited.

This can't be happening.

Chapter 7

"I'm going to have someone show you to the family room, I'll come talk to you when we know what's going on," the ICU doctor firmly directed, as I tried to make my way into the passcoded unit.

"Can I not just come with you?" I cried in panic.

"No sorry, I'll be with you as soon as I can."

"But I…"

"Tracy," she interrupted sternly, "I know this is not what you need, but we have to see to Freddie right now." She concluded hastily and she left and the heavy grey doors leading to the ICU department closed and separated us.

Andrew arrived not long later. We sat through a painful couple of hours in the family room while Freddie fought for his life. Every now and then we'd get reports on how he was doing but none of it felt like nearly enough confirmation that I wasn't about to lose my son. My baby boy, the boy I had finally connected with. Nothing would have been enough until I held him in my arms again.

Finally, after what felt like decades, the ICU doctor entered the room.

"Freddie has a nasty virus and his body is struggling to fight it. Unfortunately, we have had to intubate him," she said gently.

"Intubate, that means a ventilator, right?" Andrew interrupted.

"Yes," she confirmed.

"What does this mean, will he be ok?" I wailed in panic.

"I'm afraid we don't know that yet but the next 24 hours will be critical," she replied, before rushing back to the ICU.

We stood there frozen with shock.

"I don't have any pictures of the three boys together," I gasped out of nowhere.

"What?" Andrew responded, sounding and looking confused.

"We haven't had a chance to picture our three boys together or picture the five of us as a family. If he dies Theo and Harry will have no pictures of them with Freddie," I whispered softly.

"Tracy! Do not let your mind go there! We need to stay positive!" Andrew demanded with conviction.

Not long later, we were allowed to see Freddie. I had seen him in many medical situations before, but nothing could have prepared me for this sight. Andrew and I entered a huge, dark room, to see our tiny son lying alone in its only cot, surrounded by the hum of numerous different machines that were all hooked up to his little body. He looked so poorly and lifeless hooked up to the ventilator. His body was swollen to twice its size and his little hands were strapped to each side of the cot restraining him; I let out a breathless sob.

"Surely that is not needed! Why does he need to be restrained to a cot?" I barked to the nurse.

"It is just protocol in case he was to wake and pull the tube but we can take them off while you are here so you can hold his hands," she replied, remorsefully.

And so, we sat at opposite sides of the cot, holding his hands and willing our boy to live.

We both stayed in the hospital that night. We weren't allowed to stay in the ICU room overnight but the nurse arranged a room for us down the hall and assured us we'd be called if anything happened. We didn't get a wink of sleep that night and counted down the hours until we could be back in his room.

As we entered his room the next morning, the same doctor who had spoken to us yesterday was already there.

"Can you both come with me to the family room?" she asked.

As we followed her, Andrew gripped my hand as we glanced at one another in nervous anticipation.

"The night didn't go as well as we had hoped, Freddie is not responding to the treatment as we would have hoped and…"

"Is he going to die?!" Andrew interjected firmly. I was taken aback by his sudden directness.

"I'm afraid we have done all we can, we hope that Freddie will start to respond but…"

"IS HE GOING TO DIE?" Andrew shouted, causing me to jump.

"There is a strong chance he won't come through this, yes," she answered softly.

"Can you just give us some time alone?" I asked the doctor firmly.

As she left the room Andrew slumped to the ground in uncontrollable tears as I comforted him. "He's dying, Tracy," he sobbed.

"We need to be strong, Andrew. There is still time for him to respond to the treatment, we need to stay positive just like you said. Come on, let's go to Freddie, he needs us," I urged, surprised with my ability to not fall apart right now especially as it felt like someone had just ripped my heart out.

As we walked back into Freddie's room, we took up our seats on either side of the cot and unstrapped his hands from the blue and white velcro restraints.

"Come on Freddie, you can do this. Keep fighting, baby," I pleaded over and over.

* * *

And fight he did. What happened that afternoon was nothing short of a miracle. He started to respond; it was minor but it was positive. Ten days later, our brilliant boy, our fighter, left the ICU.

* * *

I never thought I would see the day that I'd be pleased to see Freddie back on the children's ward. I used to see this ward in such a negative light, full of sickness and low energy but after experiencing the ICU –where the line between life and death is thinner than a piece of string - it seemed brighter than it ever had and I was so grateful to be here.

Freddie's respiratory consultant, Dr Carmine, came to see us shortly after he was back on the ward.

"You are quite incredible, little man," she said to Freddie, "You must be very relieved" she turned to me, as she gripped my shoulder.

"I am, we are so proud of him for pulling through and we just want him home," I responded with a genuine smile.

"How are you feeling about him going home on oxygen?" she asked cautiously; knowing it wasn't a topic I was keen on discussing.

"You know what, I have made peace with it," I said defiantly. "It won't be forever; he's proven he's a fighter and he belongs at home with his family, so whatever we can do to make that happen we will work with you on that," I continued; knowing I meant ever word.

"Good for you," she exclaimed.

The ICU experience was the worst time of my life to date and if I could take it away and have stopped Freddie going through that I would in a heartbeat; but in a weird sort of a way it had changed me for the better. I mean here we were, a week out from Christmas and we knew we would be spending it in hospital and I wasn't having a meltdown about that.

A couple of weeks ago making peace with the fact that we would be spending Christmas in hospital – our family separated - would have been too much for me to bare and mentally I knew I would be in a very dark place. It wasn't lost on me, though, that Christmas could've been totally different in a more devastating kind of way this year if things had of taken a different turn in ICU. We could be spending Christmas without Freddie altogether and that would shatter our world. So, to have Freddie here, was a celebration in itself and this Christmas would be magical; it might not be perfect but it was good enough for us. We got our miracle, anything else was just the cherry on top.

Later that week, on Christmas Eve, while I was decorating Freddie's room with some tinsel and lights - he LOVED lights - I heard music coming from down the hall. I looked out the door and saw a parade marching through the ward. The nurses had dressed up as blown-up Christmas characters, think a festive version of sumo-suits, including Santa, an Elf and Rudolf and lapped circles of the ward holding a stereo belting out festive tunes. I took Freddie from his bed and held him at the door as we watched the parade pass our room.

As I looked up and down the hall, I could see parents and children all doing the same, full of smiles and laughter. As I took it all in, I gave silent thanks for the incredible nurses who had made such an effort to make the kids, and us parents, smile on a day that nobody wanted to be here. As I locked eyes with some other mums and dads, we gave an obligatory nod of the head and smile knowing we weren't alone. Yes, it was shit being here for Christmas, some of us separated from our other kids, but we had each other. We saw each other. And there was strength and magic in that.

* * *

The next day, Christmas Day, was hard not all being together but, with a lot of planning and help from our incredible families, we made the best of it. Andrew stayed with Freddie on Christmas Eve and early that morning my mum swapped over with him so he could be home for *Santa* with the kids. After we had breakfast, I took over from my mum and spent a few hours with Freddie and then Andrew's dad took over from me and spent the evening with him before Andrew went back in that night to stay with Freddie again. We made the best of it and Harry had the most wonderful day, which was all we were worried about most. The ICU stint had affected Harry, as myself and Andrew spent so many nights and days away from home, so it was important for us to make the Christmas build-up and the day itself as special as it could be for him and I think we succeeded.

"I must have been a good boy mummy, I got everything I wanted," he said as I tucked him into bed that night.

"You are the best boy in all the land," I whispered as he drifted off.

* * *

As Christmas and New Year's passed, it was full steam ahead for getting Freddie home from hospital. The hospital ward was so quiet over the holidays with all the consultants on Christmas break, so any plans for getting Freddie home were put on hold until January. We were okay with that though; it was nice to have some time in the hospital without doctors coming in every day and having to work my brain to digest more and more information. Having said that, when the discussions started again in early January, we were more than ready for them.

Andrew had also been working a lot in the background the last month to get us more home-help. We knew we were entitled to Jack and Jill respite hours but that was only 8 hours a week and they would only available during the daytime.

"How will we sleep at night with Freddie on CPAP, what if he stops breathing?" I would say to Andrew over and over.

"I am trying to get us more help, I am working on it," he would reply.

And work on it he did. He reached out to the Irish health minister and all local politicians campaigning for help noting the incredibly difficult journey Freddie had been on and the toll it had taken on us physically and mentally. Thankfully, his hard work paid off and we were awarded a night nurse seven nights a week for a few months to get Freddie transitioned from hospital to home. The thoughts of having someone else, someone medical, in our home every night was daunting and seemed unnatural but the thoughts of relief outweighed that and I was so thankful our application had been successful.

Andrew was so confident and passionate about advocating for Freddie, I admired him so much for that. "You just look after our boys and yourself, I'll take care of everything else," he would say. A few years ago, that statement would have offended me, I was such a strong and independent woman, I thought that meant I had to do everything, for everyone else. But this journey allowed me to soften my grip and give Andrew the space to do what he needed to support Freddie, after all he was doing it for 'our' family, not just 'mine'. I was so grateful he had the mental capacity to do it when I knew I didn't. We were growing stronger as a team every day, as we took Freddie's lead and became fighters too.

* * *

The next few weeks were a haze of paperwork and meetings to bring Freddie home. The night homecare package couldn't start until mid-February and we told the doctors we weren't confident going home without this; we had come this far what was another few weeks. They agreed and so it was just a waiting game as we continued life between home and hospital knowing there was an end in sight.

On one of these days in the hospital, I was sat on the floor with Freddie on his playmat practicing some tummy time, when a doctor and student entered the room.

"Hi mum, would it be okay if one of our students did an evaluation on Feddie as part of an exam today?" the doctor asked.

"Sure, now?" I replied.

"Yes, that would be great, could Freddie go back in his cot for it?" the doctor continued.

As I placed Freddie in the cot I asked if I could stay in the room, which they said was fine, so I pottered around tidying as they started the exam.

"Tell me what you see," the doctor said to the student.

"Hmmm, bit of an odd opener," I thought to myself.

"I see a boy of seven months old. He has dysmorphic features including a flat nose bridge, almond-shaped eyes and a shortened neck. He has…"

"EXCUSE ME?!" I interjected. "Do not speak about my child like that!"

"Um, I'm sorry? Did I do something" the student responded looking taken aback.

"Erm, you think? My son does not have distorted features…"

"She said dysmorphic not distorted," the doctor interrupted me.

"Oh right, my apologies, because that's SO much better?" I yelled back. "My son has Down Syndrome, he has some features that all people with Down Syndrome share but he is a boy first and he is not defined by his extra chromosome or his features," I continued with rage.

"Look, we will leave. Sorry to have upset you," the doctor said, sounding exasperated.

"It is 2022 and you are still teaching students to use words like dysmorphic when talking about children – babies – with Down Syndrome? Get a grip and educate yourself before you educate others," I demanded as the doctor ushered his student out the door.

As they left, I shook with anger as the tears flew down my face. I picked up Freddie and squeezed him hard, so upset that he had to be a part of some fucked up exam putting him down as a human being. Just then the door opened again and the mother from the room next door came in. She had tears in her eyes as she looked at me.

"Are you okay?" she asked kindly.

"Yes, sorry for the shouting," I said feeling embarrassed.

"Oh my god, don't be sorry. I heard the whole conversation and couldn't believe my ears. Well done you for advocating for your boy, he is lucky to have you," she responded.

Advocated. Had a just advocated? I hadn't even considered that is what I had done but I guess she was right, I had. As I digested that thought the tears came thicker and faster except this time they were tears of relief. I was enough, Freddie had been given me as his mum and I had just fought his corner for the first time. I was enough.

"Oh, I am sorry, I didn't mean to make you cry more," the other mum exclaimed as she came closer and wrapped her arms around me and Freddie. She hadn't realized my tears were no longer sad tears but I also needed that hug so I said nothing and accepted her kindness.

* * *

The day of Freddie's homecoming had finally arrived. It felt so different to bringing him home last September; that day felt like such a sad day, I hadn't bonded with Freddie then and I felt so bitter about the feeding tube that it completely took away from the joy of bringing our baby home. So, this day in February; our second chance, this day was a happy day.

Freddie's nasal feeding tube had also gone; he was still tube-fed but he now had a peg tube which was a tube that went directly into the tummy. They had decided to do it while he was in ICU in December, while he was already under sedation. It made no difference to how he was fed but because we knew the tube-feeding would be in place for some time now it made more practical sense and it made a big difference to us getting to see his gorgeous face without the tube which made him look more vulnerable and sicker than he was.

Leaving the hospital with Freddie was bittersweet. These nurses and doctors, who saw us through the worst of times, now felt like family. We had even exchanged numbers with a couple of nurses who we had bonded with so much and we genuinely felt like they loved Freddie as much as we did and we knew we would have a lifelong friendship with them. There was no mistaking it, this hospital, in particular our ward, St. Peters, held a special place in our hearts and we would forever hold gratitude to them for saving our boy's life and allowing him to come home to us.

Andrew had stuck up a picture on Freddie's wall the week we were going home. It was a picture of Freddie lying in his hospital bed beaming and Andrew had written across it in permanent marker "After 175 days, I am being evicted!". The nurses thought it was hilarious and they wanted to hang onto it as their keepsake of Freddie.

The first thing I did when we got home was take a picture of the three boys together and another of the five of us together. Looking at Harry's enormous grin as he sat centre of the sofa with a twin on either side was a sight I had longed to see; he was so happy to have Freddie home and took to our new set-up so well.

Things looked a little different this time round as we now had an oxygen canister in each room of the house along with a pump for his tube-feeding and a CPAP machine for nighttime. It was a lot to take in but once he knew what everything was for, he was satisfied and asked no more questions. It will never cease to amaze me how resilient kids can be.

We weren't going to have a night nurse that first night. We'd been all geared up to start but only the day before had been told that they could only start tomorrow night. All the hospital paperwork had been done and we were so ready for discharge day that we told them we would still go ahead and manage the first night on our own. Andrew and I knew we wouldn't sleep, so we agreed to take half the night each and stay awake with Freddie, it was only one night.

We got through the night; it had been nerve-wracking watching him on CPAP and hooked up to our portable stats monitor that controlled his vitals. We had come to see these things as so normal in the hospital but they seemed so much scarier when it's in your home and there is no doctor to call on if you are unsure about something. Still, we got through it and we would have a nurse from now on.

The next morning, the nurse from the homecare team came to visit us and meet Freddie ahead of her starting that night. Andrew answered the door and she came into the sitting room where I was sitting with Freddie.

"Hi, I'm Anne, nice to meet you," she said.

"Hi Anne. Sorry I am just a bit distracted as I am a bit worried about Freddie," I responded. Only in the last half an hour had I noticed a bit of a change in Freddie, he looked a bit pale and was lethargic too.

"Hmm, yeah he doesn't look great," she said softly, looking slightly concerned. "Have you checked his stats?"

"No not yet, this has only just happened, he was fine a little while ago," I responded.

"Okay, well let's check them then," she said as she ushered Andrew to get the monitor.

As we put the monitor on Freddie it showed his blood oxygen level was only 80%, it should be in the mid-high 90s. His colour was also rapidly getting worse and his hands and lips now had a blue tinge to them.

"Ring and ambulance now," she exclaimed firmly.

Andrew rang the ambulance as Anne cranked up his oxygen settings.

"This can't be happening. He only came home yesterday and he had a good night, we stayed up all night watching him. Why is this happening again?!" I cried in despair.

"Hey, hey just calm down, stay calm for Freddie," Anne whispered softly.

I was so thankful she was here; things had escalated so quickly I don't know how we would have reacted without her here.

By the time the ambulance arrived Freddie's colour was back to normal and he wasn't as lethargic. His blood oxygen levels had also come up to 94%.

"We are still going to bring him in," the paramedic explained.

"Yes, I know, we want to know what just happened and why," I agreed.

Thankfully, Theo and Harry weren't at home when this happened. Andrew's parents had taken Harry to school and Theo for a walk while we met with Anne.

"We're on our way to the hospital; are you okay to stay in the house for a bit?" I asked Beth on the phone.

"What do you mean, what happened?" Beth shrieked in surprise.

"We don't know, Freddie went blue. He's okay now but we need to get him checked out," I said hurriedly.

"Ok you go, we've got things covered here," she said.

* * *

"I didn't think we'd see you back here so soon!" the respiratory consultant said as she came to see Freddie in the A&E.

"Neither did we!" I explained, "what just happened?"

"We're not sure but we will keep him in tonight to monitor him," she said, eyeing us cautiously as she knew it wasn't the news we wanted.

"Ok, whatever is best for Freddie," I said, sounding deflated.

Andrew said he would stay with Freddie while I went home. I wasn't even halfway home when Andrew called me.

"He had another blue episode; we're going to ICU again," Andrew said breathlessly.

ICU again. What was happening? I turned the car and headed back for the hospital. By the time I got there he was already in ICU as I joined Andrew in the familiar surroundings of the family room.

"We have got through this once, we will get through it again," Andrew demanded.

"I know we will, I am just sad we have to do this again" I whimpered. "We were so close. We were *home*. Why is this happening?" I sobbed.

"I know, this is so unbelievably unfair but let's just take it one day at a time," Andrew grumbled.

As we went into Freddie's ICU room, we could see that he had been intubated again.

"Is it that bad?" I asked the nurse.

"We are just giving his body a bit of a break as he is working too hard but he's not where he was last time. We are hopeful he'll be ok," she said.

That is all I needed to hear. We had a reason to be positive and we had to hold onto that. This wouldn't be the same as last time, we needed to stay strong and face whatever was on the other side of this ICU admission later.

Thankfully Freddie was only in ICU for four days. The nurse was right, his body just needed a break and things didn't escalate beyond that. Once he was discharged from ICU, we made our way back to our second home - St. Peters ward.

"What in the name of God are you doing here?" exclaimed the ward manager.

"I don't know, I wish I could say it's nice to see you but I can't," I responded weakly.

"Oh love, I am so sorry," she said, as she hugged me.

The upside of being here meant I didn't feel alone in my struggles. These people knew Freddie, and us, so well at this point and we could talk with them about anything. They could understand better than our friends and family at home and I took comfort in leaning on them during this time – unsure of how long this admission might be.

I was also seeing a therapist in this hospital. Now that we were no longer inpatients of the maternity hospital, my therapy sessions with Aoife had to stop. I was so sad to lose my sessions with Aoife, she had become such an immense level of support to me and I cried bucket-loads after my last call with her but, in her final act of kindness, Aoife suggested I link in with the therapist in the children's hospital which I did and she was just as amazing.

I came to see her once a week and she awarded me that same safe, non-judgemental space that Aoife always had an I was incredibly grateful for her support.

It was after having an honest conversation and vocalizing my fears to the therapist today, that I came to a decision I knew I needed to talk to Andrew about.

* * *

"We need to have a serious chat," I told Andrew when he came in to see us that afternoon.

"What is it?" Andrew answered sounding concerned.

"I don't want to bring Freddie home until he is off oxygen," I said defiantly.

"But that could be a long time, Tracy," Andrew replied.

"I know but it's the only way to keep him safe," I cried.

We had attempted to bring Freddie home twice now. Twice it had failed. I was too scared that the third time might not end so well.

"I keep having this re-occurring nightmare," I told Andrew. "I am at home with the three boys. You are at work and I am alone. Harry needs me for something or Theo needs to be fed and I turn for five minutes and Freddie has managed to pull out his oxygen tube and he is blue. He is blue and I am alone with three kids trying to manage an emergency situation. If I am not quick enough and he dies that's on me and I would never forgive myself."

"You wouldn't be alone, Tracy," Andrew said softly.

"We can't expect your parents or my mum to continue to give up their lives to be with us all the time. We can't afford full-time nursing care in the house on one wage and we only get eight Jack and Jill hours a week. That leaves plenty of time for me to be alone with the kids and opens up the possibility of this happening," I exclaimed.

"Tracy, you are being hard on yourself. Just…"

"Admit it's a possibility?" I interrupted firmly.

"Ok it's a possibility but…"

"And how would you feel if the shoe was on the other foot and you were responsible?" I interrupted again.

"Okay" Andrew said.

"Okay, what?" I responded.

"Okay, I agree. Let's talk with the doctors," Andrew agreed, as he hugged me tightly.

* * *

The next day we asked June to call a meeting with Freddie's team where we relayed our feelings to them.

"He could be in hospital a really long time then. Do you not want him home?" Dr Nesson, Freddie's paediatrician asked.

"Of course, I do, I want nothing more. We were so excited and happy to bring Freddie home but you can't tell us what caused his blue episodes and his oxygen requirements have increased therefore you can't guarantee it won't happen again," I exclaimed. "Thank God Anne was there when this happened because I don't know how we would have handled it and if it happens again when I am alone with three kids. You tell me, how do I handle that?" I continued.

"We want Freddie home but only when we know it's safe for him and right now it doesn't feel safe," Andrew said confidently.

"Okay, well let's keep talking then and see if we can get any extra supports. I do understand," Dr Nesson said, as she gave us an emphatic nod.

I was proud of myself for standing my ground and instigating that conversation. It was hard to say I didn't want Freddie home but I knew I was doing it for the right reasons, I knew we would be sacrificing having our family all together for who knows how long but I knew deep in my gut that Freddie needed to be here and so I followed that feeling.

* * *

Another feeling I felt strongly about was that I needed to go and visit my own GP. The anxiety I was feeling lately was starting to bubble and I knew I didn't want to hit rock bottom again. I had been so good at talking and sharing my fears and worries for Freddie that I needed to honour myself with that same level of compassion and care.

Later that week I entered my GPs room prepared for a tough conversation. I hadn't seen my GP since before the twins were born so I knew she wouldn't have known the half of what's gone on.

"Wow. You have been through the mill, my love," she said with an exaggerated breath after I was done telling her all about the goings on of the last nine months. "And why do you feel like now is the right time for medication?" she asked.

"I don't know really. Back in September I was in such a bad headspace. Although I wanted it all to go away it also terrified me to not feel anything and I worried what that could do to my mental health in the long run. This time I also don't feel I need the sleeping pill support as I am managing to get sleep now. Right now, I just feel like I have this constant stream of anxiety running through my body and sometimes it feels like I am experiencing episodes of claustrophobia in my own body. Does that sound weird?" I asked.

"Not at all, what you are describing is perfectly normal and whatever you feel was right at the time was right for you," she responded gently. "I think starting you on a small dose of anti-anxiety medication is a good idea right now. It won't stop you from feeling the feelings but it will ground you a little."

Ground me. That is exactly the words I needed to hear without knowing it. Grounding – that's what I wanted to feel.

"Thank you, I am really glad I came," I said as I left the surgery with my script.

* * *

As the next few weeks passed things started to improve. Freddie continued to stay stable without catching any new infections and we managed to keep some level of family balance. We had met with our Jack and Jill coordinator to ask if we could use our 32 monthly hours while in the hospital due to our circumstances and she kindly agreed. A lot of the nurses on

Freddie's ward were Jack and Jill registered, meaning we could use them on their days off for a few hours to get some relief from the hospital. We were beyond grateful we could do that as we felt so assured when we weren't with Freddie that he was with another form of family.

We were also introduced to another organization within the hospital called *Children in Hospital Ireland*. They supported families in hospital with volunteers from the community who would come and sit or play with your child for short periods of time to give relief to parents. We were linked in with our hospital's coordinator who was so supportive and slotted in some set weekly hours for us as an additional support.

It goes without saying that we also had the full support of our families as always who pitched in wherever needed. Andrew's brother Barry lived local to the hospital and he would also come and sit with Freddie some evenings too, so Andrew and I could both be present for bedtime with the boys at home.

Our situation was far from ideal and it physically hurt not having our family under one roof but we were making the best of a bad situation and I knew that Freddie would come home to us when he was ready.

We were a family, not just us five, but an extended family; our hospital family, our charity family and our friends that were family, and between all our family we would come through this. Despite a lot of things being uncertain right now, I was beyond certain about that.

Chapter 8

As the weeks passed by, we tried to keep all the plates spinning, but it was hard to remain positive, to understand why we had been dealt this hand in life. I asked myself that question every day, and I was finally awarded an answer, one that came in the form of signs.

I was never a real believer in the "universe" but that changed one day while I was on my way home from the hospital. As I drove, I listened to an episode of *The Good Glow with Georgie Crawford*. It had been a while since I'd tuned in to the podcast, even though it was something I'd been religious about enjoying before this chaos had descended on our world. As I tuned in, Georgie introduced her American guest, Gabby Bernstein, author of *The Universe Has Your Back*, and the more I heard the more my body said 'YEEESSSS'.

Not long into the episode, Gabby explained that we can ask the universe a question and it will answer with a sign to let us know we're on the right track. Ordinarily, I wouldn't have thought much about this, believing it was some "woo woo" ideology that didn't exist in the real world, but for some reason today it struck something inside me and I thought;" what do

I have to lose? "So, I switched off the podcast and wracked by brain for a question to ask. I couldn't find the words; in fact, I didn't really know what I was asking for. So, instead of complicating it I kept it really simple and as I drove the last stretch home on a dreary March Day, I asked the universe for my first sign.

"I'm starting to think that this whole experience has been for a reason, that Freddie will come home to us and we'll all be stronger because of this. I am not sure what the lesson is but I think there might be a lesson at the end of all of this. If I am right, I ask for a sign in the form of... *a sunflower,*" I said aloud.

I felt silly saying it, I don't know where the sunflower idea came from but I had put it out there and if there was really something to this then I guessed I would soon find out.

About 10 minutes later, as I neared home, I had the instinct to look up. As I did, I saw the usual big green road sign to my left indicating how many kilometres I was from various towns. I was so accustomed to seeing this sign as I drove by it daily but today, I saw something different; something I had never noticed before. Sitting right at the top of this sign, as clear as day, was a picture of.... *A SUNFLOWER!!*

"No bloody way!" I said aloud to myself in disbelief. I was so convinced that I'd imagined the image that I turned the car around at the next exit and went back just so I could drive by it again. There was no mistaking it, it was a sunflower.

Something inside me changed in that moment; this was all happening for a reason and I had to trust the process – trust the universe. For the first time in a long time, I felt genuine hope and reassurance, and I knew I just needed to hold on a little while longer.

My mum was home with the two boys when I got in a little while later, I contemplated telling her about my sign but soon decided against it. I decided against telling anyone close to me about the sunflower. I was afraid they might say it was silly and I was afraid that I might believe them. I didn't want to believe that; the positive feelings it brought me were not something I wanted to abandon.

"Would you mind if I went for a quick walk before you go? It's been a long day and I just need some air," I asked my mum.

"Sure, take your time," she replied.

As I walked out the door, I started to question if the sunflower sign really was silly? I had never believed things like this before, was I just using this as a crutch to lean on? And would I suffer the consequences of a hard fall if I leaned too hard on it? Maybe I had seen that sunflower on the road sign before and my subconscious mind knew I was going to see it soon? As I fought my thoughts, another instinct rose inside me telling me to look to my left. As I followed the feeling, I turned my head and saw the familiar big red-brick building of the primary school that sat at the end of our road. As I kept walking by it, I looked closer and what stared back at me honestly took my breath away. Sitting inside one of the large glass windowpanes starting directly out towards me where paintings of about 20 vibrant yellow sunflowers.

The tears came thick and heavy as I stopped and looked at them. There was no mistaking it; this was my sign and I had to pay attention.

Everything was going to be ok. I decided there and then: Today will be the last day I doubt that. Today, I surrender and trust the process.

* * *

As I moved forward, I felt more hopeful than I ever had before. Things might be hard, but I knew it would all work out for the better, so I could relax a little. I felt different, stronger, but when I looked in the mirror the wear and tear of the last year told a different story. I didn't recognize myself. Yes, I had made the important decision to go on medication for my anxiety and it was working just like my doctor said it would, I felt grounded but still very much aware of my feelings and emotions – something I was afraid of losing - but going on the medication at the time I did had been a reaction to the overwhelm; a direct response to the moment I was in. It was a band-aid, a much-needed band-aid, but I now realized I needed so much more.

After growing twins for near seven months, breastfeeding and eating every meal on the go with little to no exercise, I had gained weight and I didn't feel good about myself. I had stopped doing all the things that made me happy. I used to sea swim daily, I used to work out two to three times a week, my body missed feeling the cold Irish sea on its skin, it missed the feeling of strength the gym gave me. Things had to change. I vowed to take more time for myself, I knew now that self-care wasn't a luxury – it was survival.

The next morning, before I went to the hospital, I drove the 10 minutes from my house to my favourite swim spot, *The Cove* in Greystones.

As I stepped in, the first sting of cold water took my breath away. My skin screamed, begging me to run back to the car, but I persevered and sank myself down into the salty blue sea.

I let it wash over me and was rewarded with that feeling I'd come to love so much since I started sea-swimming two years ago. The cold water had washed me clean of worry. It's like a rebirth, for the mind and body, and I walked back out of the water a little different.

A little bit braver.

A little bit stronger.

A little bit happier.

A lot more alive.

I had missed her, the me that the Irish sea returned me to. I would never forget her again.

* * *

Stepping foot back in the gym wasn't as easy, I had such fear of being judged.

"I don't know if I can do it. People will think I am so selfish being in the gym while Freddie is in hospital" I said to my friend Helen one day over a cuppa.

"Listen here, you are an amazing mum and I am so proud of you. You need to do this for you, screw what anyone else thinks but I can guarantee you people will only have praise for you – like I do" she said as she squeezed my hand.

I knew I had to do it, I had to do it for my mental health and that was more important than what anyone might think of me. I had been doing some research online about maternal mental health recently, something I have become increasingly passionate about as a result of my recent sufferings, and some of the facts shocked me.

I was particularly intrigued by a study only just completed

by *Trinity's school of Nursing and Midwifery* which followed the prevalence of, and changes over time in, depression, anxiety and stress-symptoms experienced by first-time mothers. The study has been published in the journal *Archives of women's mental health*.

The key findings of this study showed that one in ten women reported symptoms of moderate to severe anxiety in their first year postpartum and one in seven women reported moderate to severe depression symptoms, while one in five women reported moderate stress to severe stress symptoms also in the first year postpartum.

The study also showed that although more conversations are now happening around mental health there is still very much a stigma and silence that surrounds mental health problems.

Although I could relate to feeling this, I knew it wasn't right and vowed to speak up about this – through my experience – when the time was right.

Despite my fear and reservations, I needn't have been worried about returning to the gym. I was only met with kindness and compassion, and praised for setting some time aside for looking after myself. I realised I was surrounded by other mothers, who knew just what this ritual meant. They knew I was reclaiming myself.

And that was the long and short of it really. I wasn't not going to the hospital to be with my son. I wasn't not looking after my babies at home. I wasn't taking advantage of others minding my children while I was out having the time of my life. I was taking an hour a day to mind myself and that hour would benefit everybody around me.

My boys will have a happier and more patient mum.

My husband will have a wife that isn't so resentful of him still having his career.

My family will get a part of their daughter, sister and daughter-in-law back.

My friends will hear from me a little more.

I will come back to me.

These thoughts ran through my mind every time I stepped inside the gym. It was my own personal reminder that what I was doing was of benefit. To me, firstly, but also to all those in my life.

The treadmill that surely was stuck on a tougher setting than it used to be. The weights that were clearly heavier. The rowing machine that mustn't have been oiled in a while. At every step of every work out, as my out-of-shape body fought against how 'hard' this was, I reminded myself why I needed it. I reminded myself of my breakdown only months ago. I reminded myself of my little fighter Freddie, who had been through so many challenges, and yet still kept going. If he could push through the discomfort, so could I.

My gym sessions became far less about what I 'should' do for my body, and far more about what I 'choose' to do for my health. My mindset shifted dramatically and the mothers around me cheered me on.

During this time, I was also introduced to a woman in my community called Mary. Mary is a breathwork coach and practiced *the Wim Hof method*. I had always been interested in breathwork and heard the many benefits of it but always figured it was something "I didn't have time for".

I reached out to Mary on Instagram and asked her how I could learn more. She told me she was holding a class the following evening and I should come along so I did.

I was really blown away by Mary and her teachings. The breathwork wasn't at all what I was expecting, I thought it would be really relaxed and meditative but this was what she calls "active breathwork" and it was a bit of a workout if I am being honest but the "do-er" in me liked that.

The feelings I had during the breathwork session amazed me, I felt empowered, alive and full of energy. It was truly incredible and I vowed to keep up with regular sessions.

* * *

With this renewed sense of confidence giving me some much-needed strength back, I decided to visit a good friend of mine. Mary is a craniosacral therapist and I had been going to her for treatment since I was about 17. Craniosacral therapy is a therapy that uses light physical touch to release tension around your body's connective tissue network. Not only is Mary an incredible therapist but she is the most wonderfully positive person and her energy is infectious.

Truth was, I had been putting off visiting Mary for some time now. She was one of those people who could see right through me, and until then, I wasn't ready to break down on her therapy bed, I wasn't ready to have the emotional release I knew her treatment would give me.

As I walked into Mary's therapy room in Dublin, she embraced me in the warmest and tightest hug imaginable and the tears came immediately.

"You are one bloody strong woman and I am so proud of you," she told me as she gripped my shoulders and looked me straight in the eyes before embracing me again.

The treatment was wonderful and I immediately felt lighter after it. I hadn't realized the level of tension that was trapped in my body until it was gone and I inwardly scolded myself for waiting this long to come.

It wasn't just the treatment that had made me feel lighter, it was just being in Mary's company. She was a huge believer in the universe, signs and manifesting. She was completely flabbergasted when I told her about my sunflower sign and her excitement and encouragement solidified my own feeling.

"That boy is going to surprise us all. He is a fighter and he is making you a fighter too. Embrace it. The hard times you are going through right now will be your superpower," she said defiantly as I left four hours later.

* * *

The longer I sat with the thought that this was all happening for a reason, I started to wonder if there were any lessons showing up that I was missing? I was so focused on the end goal and what teachings lay for me there, but did I even know what the end goal was? Would I wake one day and suddenly realize "Oh that's the end of that now"? I suspected not. So, instead I tried to think about what this experience had taught me so far. When I sat down with a notebook, and journalled my thoughts, I was surprised with what came out. I realised the change wouldn't come once we made it through the hard times, the change was happening now, as we took the journey. I started to list what I had learnt so far:

I have learnt it's okay to be a mum and to still be me.
I have learnt that worrying too much about the future does

not serve you. Whatever life has in store for us is going to happen anyway, worrying about that is not going to stop it happening, so I shouldn't waste so much energy on it.

I have learnt that looking after your mental health is as important as looking after your physical health.

I have learnt that there is huge power and strength in asking for help. I might fear that I am a burden but I might just find people are only too happy to be asked to help; to feel like they are part of your journey.

I have learnt that self-care doesn't look like holidays, spa days or shopping trips. Self-care to me now is a sea swim, 30 minutes in the gym, a brisk walk with a podcast. Self-care is whatever makes me feel like me and what makes my soul sing.

I have learnt that having gratitude, even in the darkest of days, will get me through and keep hope alive.

Most importantly, I have learnt that even while I am still on this journey, I have already been given the greatest gift. The gift to live in the present. The road Freddie has brought us on has meant life had to be taken hour by hour and not day by day or month by month. At one point an hour was all it took to be closer to life than death and if that's not perspective I don't know what is. I used to be an over-planner, needing to know what was happening a week ahead all the time but Freddie has given me the gift of learning to slow down. I don't need to have it all figured out all the time and the pressure that relieves is immeasurable.

I had my sign; I knew I was on the right path but instead of waiting for the train to reach its destination I needed to embrace the ride and take in the scenery all around me because the lessons didn't lie at the last stop; there were lessons to be learned at every stop.

***

Another thing that I had really learnt over the past few months was how powerful connections can be. Andrew and I had connected with a lot of people over the last while and it never ceased to amaze me how incredible human connection really is.

We were so lucky to have been surrounded by family and friends but it was people that came out of the woodwork that surprised me most: old friends that came back into our lives offering support; new friends that were made through sharing experiences; hospital workers; Harry's pre-school teachers; friends of friends; and strangers in the Down Syndrome community who all rallied and lifted us up when we needed it.

My best friend Nicola has been the greatest support to me over the last year, sometimes there are things you just don't want to say to your husband or mum and so Nicola was always my listening ear when I wanted to have the more uncomfortable conversations when you need someone who is just that little bit more removed from the situation.

Nicola also has a friend called Laura, they were childhood friends and although I had met Laura once or twice, I never really got to know her that well but over the last year she has made such an effort to support me and my family. She only lives a few minutes from the children's hospital and offered on many occasions to come and have a chat or drop me dinner. She is a mum too with a young son so I guess she could put herself in my shoes and somehow imagine just how hard my life was right now but her support and kindness meant more than she could have known. Myself, Laura and Nicola have become such a close trio over the last year. they are my true soul sisters and I am so grateful for them.

With all the kindness shown to me, I vowed to do more for other people when our life was more stable. I had been so touched and felt so grateful for every act of kindness we received and I knew I wanted to give that back somehow when the timing was right.

Although all these outside connections meant to much, I knew it was also so important to honour and nurture the connections closest to us and for me my closest connection was Andrew.

Andrew and I had become like ships in the night over the past while. I knew we were both still there underneath it all but I started to understand how relationships can break down in times like this. I was grateful that I had the insight to be able to acknowledge this and have the honest conversations about it.

We took some time-out one evening in March for our fourth wedding anniversary and went to our favourite pizza restaurant in Dublin, Paulies. It was there that I shared my fears and worries with Andrew; my hope that we would make it through this – together.

"We are going through an incredibly unique time in our life right now. We still love each other and support each other; we will get through this," Andrew reassured me.

I was worried Andrew would resent me for taking some time for myself every day, time that he didn't get to take but he assured me that wasn't the case. He was proud of me for making myself a priority and he did take some time out now and again to see his friends but for now work was his escape, he loved his job and was so passionate about it and it needed him.

Truth be told our business had taken a bit of a hit the last while as our foot was understandably taken off the pedal but we were so incredibly thankful for our team of staff who kept the ship sailing in our absence; I don't think our business would have survived without them and we made a point to always tell them how much we appreciated them. They were another connection that were so important to us and supported us like family.

* * *

Before I immersed myself back into the conversations around Freddie's next homecoming, I decided to book myself into a half-day retreat with a wellness psychologist I had been following on Instagram. Her name was Dr Clodagh Campbell and she was a psychologist who had a more holistic approach to therapy and healing journeys; her message really spoke to me and I could always really relate to her content.

One of the things Clodagh spoke about at the retreat that really stuck with me was a metaphor she used for looking after what is important to us. She said we all have glass balls and plastic balls in life. Our plastic balls are the little everyday things; if we drop a plastic ball it's okay, we can pick it up again. Our glass balls are more precious, they symbolize what really matters to us in life and we must nurture and protect them so we don't drop and shatter them.

It was such an a-ha moment for me. My glass balls were Andrew and my boys, my friends, my family and my self-care; I needed to mind them. We needed to mind each other. My plastic balls were just filler in my life and they would be dropped whenever needed to ensure I always kept my glass balls afloat.

The day was just what I needed and more than I could have hoped for; it grounded me in a way I hadn't felt before and I left feeling truly at peace with what was to come next for me.

* * *

Piece by piece, gratitude by gratitude, I started to see the bigger picture and return to myself again. Each strand in my self-care system was important. The sign from the universe, the sea-swimming, the gym sessions, the five-minute moments throughout the day when I just paused and focused on my breath. They were all tools in my self-care first-aid kit. All re-energizing my weary body and mind, transforming me into the woman I was becoming.

I remember reading a beautiful story once before about flamingos and how when they have their babies, they lose their vibrant pink colour and turn a pale pink or white while they feed and raise their babies but, once their babies grow, they regain their pink back.

And now, amidst all the chaos in my life; I really started to feel like I was getting my pink back.

Chapter 9

As I sat on the stoney, pebbled beach of The Cove, watching the sunrise after an early morning dip, I gave silent gratitude for being here, for being so lucky to call this town home and having the sea on my doorstep. The sun warmed my back with those first rays of summer making their presence felt. It was May, we were on the cusp of summer, and I hoped that one day soon Freddie would be joining us on the beach, breathing in that glorious sea air. Soon.

I could have sat there all day, but remembering I was headed straight for the hospital to see my boy as he woke gave me all the motivation I needed to move.

As I walked into Freddie's room, I was pleased to see he was still sleeping. I never liked the thought of him waking without one of us there but our hospital admission had been so long at this point there was no way we could stay every night now that Andrew was back working full-time. We tried our best to do three or four nights a week and on the nights we couldn't do we had to make peace with the fact that the nurses would mind him. We were lucky that Freddie slept all night so on most occasions, after we would put him to sleep at night, he would sleep until we returned in the morning.

Freddie started to stir as I busied myself in his room restocking nappies and clothes. "Good morning, baby boy," I said as I lifted him from his cot for the first cuddle of the day. I was greeted with the biggest grin in response. When Freddie was sick the lows could be very low but when he was stable, like he was now, he just radiated joy and I wondered how I got so lucky to call this ray of light mine.

After our morning routine of a bath, followed by some play and physio, I put his tube-feed on as we settled down in the recliner chair for some cuddles and stories. Freddie loved his cuddles, especially after doing some physio, which tired him quickly. As we sat in the chair together, I wondered how much longer we would have to do this for. I knew it couldn't be good for Freddie to continue to developmentally grow in a hospital environment, he needed nurturing in a home environment, but our experience of bringing Freddie home – twice – had been so traumatic I feared the same thing happening again. "There has to be a way to make this work", I thought.

As I looked down at Freddie in my arms, gazing at me so hard it was like he was searching deep into my soul, I made him a promise; a promise I knew I had to keep. "Whatever it takes I am going to fight for you to have the happiest and healthiest life. I don't know how it's going to look, or how we are going to make it work, but I promise I won't let you down. You have shown us how much you want to be here by fighting as hard as you have. I promise to bring you home to us as soon as I can," I said softly, choking back the tears that were threatening so hard to expose themselves.

I went home later that evening after getting Freddie to sleep; Andrew had kept the boys up a little later so I could see them before bed. As I tucked them in after reading a story, I went downstairs to Andrew who had dinner waiting for me.

"I am going to go in and give Freddie a goodnight kiss, I will be back soon," he said as I began to eat.

"Could it wait a while? I want us to talk first," I asked.

"What's wrong?" Andrew asked cautiously, as he took up a seat beside me at the kitchen island.

Andrew always got nervous whenever I said I needed to talk. He has had to deal with many emotional breakdowns from me; I think he thought another was on the way.

"It's not good for Freddie being stuck in the hospital long-term, we need to do more to get him back to us," I said.

"I know but what can we do? We've said we can't take him home until he is off breathing support. We don't know how long that is going to be," Andrew responded. "We have always said we only have two options – bring him home and hope the same thing doesn't happen again or keep doing what we are doing between home and hospital until he comes off oxygen," he continued sounding exasperated that we were having the same conversation again.

"What if there is a third option?" I offered.

"Go on..." Andrew replied slowly and cautiously.

"I have been reading online about fostering..."

"YOU WANT TO GIVE FREDDIE UP?" Andrew barked.

"Let me finish," I replied softly, swallowing hard before saying what I was about to say. "It's called voluntary fostering. Freddie would go to a family who can support him in a home environment the way we can't with the other kids. They could give him their undivided attention and nurture him until he comes off oxygen. We would still have contact and be able to see him but they would be his primary caregivers until we can bring him home."

"I'm not sure, Tracy, how could we let Freddie be with another family? He is our boy, he is a twin, we can't separate him from us," Andrew said softly with tears in his eyes.

"What's the alternative? He comes home here, pulls out his oxygen when I am tending to one of the other kids and has a respiratory attack and I have to deal with a medical emergency on my own with two other kids here? We cannot ask family to give up their lives to be here with me. We can't afford full-time nursing care in the house. What is the alternative? I hate this idea too but I am just thinking about what is best for Freddie. It breaks my heart to think what is best for him might not be with us right now but it wouldn't be forever." I cried which soon led to sobs.

"Shhhh, it's ok," Andrew whispered. "I know you are only thinking of Freddie's best interests. Let's discuss this more with June and see what she thinks?"

I nodded in response.

* * *

The next day we both went to the hospital and after spending some time with Freddie, we asked June to meet with us. Usually when we have chats with her, it's in Freddie's room with him present, but it didn't feel right having this conversation around Freddie, so instead, we asked to meet in her office.

"So, what can I do for you both?" she asked.

"We are considering the option of voluntary fostering for Freddie and we would like your advice on it," I said, sounding more confident than I was feeling.

"Okay, what made you come to this decision?" she responded kindly.

"We don't want to see Freddie staying in hospital any longer than he needs to but we are so fearful bringing him home that we can't keep him safe; our two past experiences have taught us that. We want Freddie to be loved and nurtured and ideally, we would be the people to do that, but maybe someone else could do it in the interim – until he is off oxygen. We still want to see Freddie and be connected to him and we want him home to us eventually, that's why we looked into the voluntary fostering," I said nervously, aware that this idea was now no longer just between myself and Andrew but instead out in the open.

"You are right, there is such a thing as voluntary fostering and you will still be able to see Freddie but it can be a long process to get to the point of having Freddie placed. I suggest we have another multi-disciplinary team meeting with Freddie's care-providers to discuss this as a team. Are you okay with this?" she asked.

We both nodded in agreement.

* * *

The next day we walked into the MDT with nervous anticipation. What would the outcome of this meeting be? Were we truly awful parents for even considering this? So many questions flooded my mind but I knew I owed it to Freddie to explore every option to give him the best possible chance of getting out of hospital.

As we walked into the room a little while later my stomach did somersaults knowing this conversation was really happening; it was no longer just a thought or an idea. As we took up our seats at the opposite side of the large table in the boardroom, it felt like we were attendees at an interview.

"Why do you want to consider voluntary fostering?" Dr Nesson asked.

"It was my idea, I brought it to Andrew. I don't think Andrew is fully set on the idea but he understands why I might want to do it. When Freddie comes home, I will be his main carer, I will have two other kids to look after too and I have this constant reoccurring nightmare of Freddie dying at home," I exclaimed, knowing now was not the time to sugarcoat things.

"I fear that Freddie might pull out his oxygen while I'm not looking and have a respiratory attack and go blue again. We cannot afford full-time nursing care; we cannot expect our parents to always be with us. Andrew's parents are retired and in their 70's, my mum works full-time, and we'll only get maximum eight hours a week support from Jack and Jill. We're so grateful for all the support we've been offered but it still leaves too many gaps where something can happen and I cannot live knowing I could be the reason Freddie dies. I want Freddie home with us more than anything but I want what is best for him more. It is so hard to admit that I think right now what is best for him is not in our home because I can't offer him my devoted attention with two other boys to take care of at the same time. I just want him to be safe, I have never wanted anything more," I wailed.

"I wasn't sure about the idea when Tracy first said it," Andrew followed up. "I was shocked she had looked into it but the more she explains why she did, the more I understand and I agree it's worth considering."

"If you do this you see it being until Freddie is off oxygen, right?" a respiratory consultant on Freddie's team asked.

We both nodded in unison.

"You know, we don't know how long Freddie might need oxygen for but in some cases, it can be four or five years. You do know that?" she continued.

"Well, no, that has never been said before. Why weren't we told this before?" I asked in panic.

"Every case is different and we truly do not know how long he will need it for but there have been cases where children with lung diseases have been on it that long. I just want to make sure you are aware of that," she answered sympathetically.

"I think next steps would be for us to contact Tusla. They are the country's child and family care agency; they monitor child safety and place kids with foster families. We can set-up a meeting with them and you to discuss further what might be involved in doing this," Dr Nesson interrupted. "As you know this process could take a long time if you went through with it but they can talk more with you about that."

"Ok, let's do that. Thank you for hearing us," I said before we both got up to leave.

"Why don't you sit outside for a minute, I'll come chat to you then," Mae said.

As we sat outside, I felt equal parts relieved to have had the conversation and sad that the conversation needed to be had. Why did doing something that felt like was for the greater good feel so bad? My gut was screaming at me that this didn't feel right. As I was about to say that to Andrew, Mae joined us.

"You all saying what awful parents we are in there?" I joked to Mae; we had that kind of relationship with her, like we could say anything and she just *got* us.

"No. We were saying how brave you are. I don't think you realize just how much strength it takes to come in and have that conversation. You are far from awful parents; you are amazing parents," she exclaimed.

"I only want what is best for Freddie," I said softly.

"And that absolutely came across," Mae smiled, as she gripped my hand.

When we went back to Freddie's room Andrew sat him on his knee, as I took up space on the chair beside them.

"I can't do it," I said.

"What?" Andrew replied

"The fostering. I can't go through with it. My gut is telling me it's not right. I needed to speak it, I needed to explore it and ask the questions. I needed to know I had explored it for Freddie's sake but walking out of that room, I knew it was wrong," I said firmly.

"But what about everything you said? Not being able to cope at home, which is valid and true and hasn't changed," Andrew questioned.

Something came to me after the meeting, something I had read recently that struck a chord. In life we get to choose our hard. For example, getting fit is hard but being unhealthy is hard; we choose our hard. There were lots of other examples but the point for me is bringing Freddie home on breathing support would be hard but giving him up to another family, letting them be responsible for his care would be hard; actually, it would be a million times harder so that's why I couldn't do it.

When I explained this to Andrew, he got it.

"I am really proud of you. You are an amazing mum and our boys are so lucky to have you," Andrew said.

The next day we told the team not to make the Tusla referral and they agreed.

***

Over the next few weeks, we made a lot of progress and it finally felt like things were moving, we were no longer stuck in a state of limbo and it felt like there was a different energy about the hospital now. It was like speaking about my fears and exploring the fostering alternative expelled something from my body and cleared the stagnant energy that we'd been living through for so long and made space for change to start.

I had a fire in my belly that was bursting to get out and I was honouring it. Freddie's teams were surprised at our quick change of heart but understood it was something we needed to get off our chests and they accepted and agreed it wasn't something we needed to move forward with. They were also surprised that not only had we abandoned the fostering idea but that we wanted to start the talks on Freddie coming home – even on oxygen.

"What's changed? You were so fearful of something happening at home?" Dr Nesson asked.

"I still am, it terrifies me, but other people have obviously done it so we can too. I am not too proud to ask for every bit of help I can get to get us through this. Freddie needs to be home; it is not serving him being here," I explained confidently.

"Well, we will support you in whatever way we can," Dr Nesson replied as she gently patted my shoulder.

After consulting with the night homecare team, we soon had a date for a homecoming: July 6. It was just over a month away but enough time to get plans in place and do our best to set up for success. Maybe this will be third time lucky? I hoped with every fibre of my being that it would be.

There was another milestone approaching much sooner that that though. We were only days away from the twins first birthday. I couldn't quite believe it had been a year. In some ways, it felt like only yesterday and in other ways it felt like a lifetime ago.

A year…

A year in hospital with our boy.

A year of my baby twins being separated.

A year since I became a different version of myself.

A year since my experience of motherhood starkly changed.

A year of pain, grief and hopelessness but also a year of joy, miracles and much hope.

I wondered how so many feelings could co-exist together. How you could feel hopelessness and hope with such short pockets of space in between. But you can; I am a living example that you can and the feeling that ties them all together is one that I am most thankful for: Gratitude.

Being grateful in times of hopelessness led me to reasons to have hope.

Being grateful in times of despair led to miracles happening.

Being grateful when I experienced pain led me to feeling joy.

There were always reasons to be grateful, I might have had to dig a little harder to find it sometimes but it's always there and I would forever carry that forward with me.

Being grateful also helped me get through the boys first birthday. They arrived into this world together, it's only natural they should celebrate every birthday side by side, so it was hard to come to terms with the fact that they wouldn't get to be together on this one. But weren't we still lucky? We were close to Freddie coming home to us again and he was gaining in strength all the time. He might still be on oxygen and tube-feeding but he is a far-cry from where he was.

Millie, one of his nurses, was on duty on his birthday and she decorated his room with banners and balloons and made a real fuss of him – and us – but it was the arrival of the birthday cake and all the St. Peters nursing team descending on our room singing "Happy Birthday" that tipped me over the edge as I sobbed into Freddie's chest while I held him in my arms. Our boy was so loved that much was clear.

We had decided to delay celebrating the boys' birthday, until Freddie was home, but the fuss the hospital made of Freddie made me feel guilty for not celebrating Theo, so that evening we had the family round and had more cake and singing to celebrate our other miracle boy. The boy who healed my mama heart on days it was breaking, the boy who took the last year in his stride with a smile on his face always. People would often ask how hard it must be having twins with one poorly in hospital and there is no doubt about it, it's heartbreaking, but I guess I know no different and having Theo to spend my non-hospital days with and having him to come home to and cuddle at night helped take the pain of the day away. Knowing you have a sick baby can consume you with worry but coming home to a well and thriving baby restores faith again.

Sometimes it makes me sad to know that I can't relate to most other twin moms. I don't know what it's like to bring two babies home together and manage the tandem feeding and the overwhelm of meeting both babies demands at the same time, but I know I was given both my boys at the same time for a reason; they were both playing their parts that moulded me into the mother I was evolving into and I was so grateful for our unique twins.

* * *

Four days before Freddie was due to come home, we were dealt a blow we didn't see coming. The homecare team could no longer facilitate this start date and instead wanted to start the following week.

"No, you can't do this, we have been working towards this date for weeks now. Andrew has the week off work, we need to maximize our time home as a family," I barked at Karen, our homecare facilitator.

"I am so sorry, the nurse we had lined up is sick, there is nothing we can do," she replied solemnly.

"I can't change my week off in work. Let's just try bringing him home without their help," Andrew offered.

"No way. We need this transition to go smoothly. Our confidence with bringing Freddie home needs to be built, we need the support," I demanded.

"Ok, well I guess we need to wait then," Andrew shrugged.

"No, he is coming home 6 July. It is happening, I will sort this," I said defiantly. I wasn't backing down on this, nobody was taking this away from us, not now when we were so close.

I got straight on the phone to Fiona, our Jack and Jill coordinator. We had been getting 32 care hours a month in the hospital and we would continue to get these hours at home. We'd already been linked with two nurses in our hometown, Jane and Orla, who would support us at home for some day hours, in four-block periods. I told Fiona about our predicament and how devastated we were that the goalpost had been moved on us.

"Andrew has the week off work booked, I really need that support initially so I was wondering would the Jack and Jill foundation be able to give us some hours so we can get a night nurse in for the first week at home?" I asked hopefully

"Of course, we'll give you extra hours, we are here to help however we can but I don't think Jane or Orla could do the nights," Fiona said.

"I'll ask our nurses here in the hospital. I will make it happen I just need the hours. We would be so grateful," I exclaimed.

"I'll give you the seven nights of hours no problem," Fiona responded compassionately.

With this confirmed, I got to work and talked to all the nurses on Freddie's ward to see if any of them would be interested. A lot of them were and within an hour I had the seven-night roster done between Freddie's ward nurses and Jane. I soon realized this hiccup was a blessing; Freddie would now come home and have nurses he knew and was so accustomed to for the first week and it was reassuring for us too.

Once everything was planned and our home plan was back on track, I felt an overwhelming sense of pride. I was proud of myself, instead of backing down and accepting our fate of a later discharge I stood my ground and advocated for our family, something I wouldn't have had the strength to do a few months ago. I really started to believe I could do this.

Andrew stayed in with Freddie on 5 July and after getting the boys to bed, I spent an hour in Freddie's room making sure everything was perfect for our boy. I had picked out clothes to bring into the hospital in the morning to bring him home in; a blue and white mickey mouse vest with a pair of short denim dungarees over them. It had been months since I had dressed Freddie in anything other than baby grows, so the simple joy of picking out clothes for him meant so much.

As I sat on the floor in the centre of his room gripping the clothes, the silent tears dropped from my eyes onto the beige carpet.

"You are coming home, baby. You are coming home."

Leaving hospital the next day, I felt so emotional and struggled to keep my emotions in check. This ward and these people meant so much to us. They had been the extended family we never knew we needed and showed us so much love and kindness that never went unnoticed. We would never forget them and they would always hold the most special place in our hearts.

As we walked out the door of the hospital the biggest rainbow greeted us. Although not "my sign", I knew it was "a sign". This time it was right, everything was going to be alright.

* * *

The first few weeks being home went really smoothly. Having the hospital nurses for the first few nights was such a reassuring experience. When the homecare team took over, we were relieved to immediately bond with our night nurse Sheila who lived local to us and had four boys of her own, including a set of twins, so she immediately knew the chaos that now existed in our home.

The boys adored having Freddie home, Harry loved being the protective older brother and Theo enjoyed having a playmate who didn't get bored of him after 10 minutes!

The worry of the oxygen and feeding routines wasn't as daunting now we were home, he was definitely stronger than he was the last time he came home and we had a good system of help without asking too much of any one individual.

It was only after these initial few weeks home that a new reality started to dawn on us.

Freddie has Down Syndrome.

When Freddie was first born his diagnosis overshadowed every thought I had. Then when he had his first ICU admission and we were told he may not make it, I remember thinking back to that day when they were born. It had seemed like the end of the world but now sitting in ICU with my very sick baby I wished that all I had to deal with was him having Down Syndrome. It seemed so insignificant in the grand scheme of things and ultimately having Down Syndrome was a part of Freddie that made him who he was and I now wouldn't change that for the world.

Now that we were home and had some sort of routine, we needed to row back to dealing with Freddie's Down Syndrome diagnosis and get him the supports to enable him to live his best and most fulfilling life.

Shortly after Freddie was born, I had been linked in with a local support group of mums who all had children with Down Syndrome in my hometown. There were about 15 mums with kids ranging from newborns to eight years old. It was lovely to connect with them and feel less alone but I didn't interact much initially feeling like I didn't belong as my baby was so unwell.

Now that we were settled at home, I vowed to make more of an effort and really connect with these mums and children that would likely become lifelong friends of Freddie.

Once I put myself out there, I was in awe of what I received back; so many of the other mums offering kindness, advice and support and guiding me forward in how and what supports to access for Freddie. Connecting with these amazing women gave me such a sense of belonging, this was a tribe I belonged in.

"Tracy, you need to visit the Down Syndrome Centre in Dublin" said Niamh enthusiastically, one of the other mums I had grown particularly close to. Niamh had a boy the same age as my twins and coincidently her boy was called Theo!

"Honestly, it is so empowering. The future is bright for our boys, I promise you!" she continued.

I had never heard of the Centre before but going by Niamh's roaring recommendation, I decided to do a bit of research on it.

I learned that The Down Syndrome Centre was set up by Peter and Mary Gaw as a result of their frustration at not being able to access relevant services for their two youngest children, both of whom have Down Syndrome. In 2014, they opened the doors to Ireland's first services-led centre for children with Down Syndrome and their families. I emailed them right away and arranged to come and visit the Centre with Andrew and the three boys.

Walking into the Down Syndrome Centre a few days later was an experience I will never forget. It is beautiful environment filled with bright colours, fish tanks, a wonderfully calming sensory room filled with lava lamps and plush beanbags, a therapy-based gym and fun, welcoming therapy rooms for physiotherapy, occupational therapy and speech and language therapy. They also host playgroups for the kids, so families can connect in a safe and non-judgmental space.

Everybody we met in the Centre greeted us with a warm smile. This place was special and I immediately felt at home. How lucky were we that this place not only existed but that it was practically on our doorstep? Another reason to be oh so grateful.

As a child with a disability, Freddie was already entitled to free therapy services within our community to support him as he grew up so I prior to visiting the centre I wondered if we really needed the support of them but after visiting, I just knew it would be a place we would visit often; the energy and optimism in the centre was infectious and we truly felt like it was a place to belong. The community therapists were lovely but it felt very focused on disability and the services were very stretched meaning there were long wait periods to be seen and assessed but the centre felt far from this – yes it was there to support children with their disability - but it was focused on doing this in the most relaxed, fun and inclusive way and celebrating that not everyone is the same and being different is okay and accepted.

The Centre's motto is "A Place to Thrive" and I really felt like that was true. With the support of the Down Syndrome Centre, Freddie would thrive, we would all thrive.

For the first time in a long time, I looked at our future with excitement. There would be challenges along this road, I was sure of that, but we had been through the worst and I was determined to give Freddie – to give all our boys – the best childhood we could.

Chapter 10

Come Autumn 2022, life was vastly different to what it had been the previous year. We were home and had stayed home. Our confidence in looking after Freddie and his medical needs while also looking after our other two children and managing our business was growing. It wasn't easy but we were doing it and Freddie was thriving. Everyone basked in the joy of watching him start this new chapter in his little life.

We couldn't get over the change in Freddie since being home. Initially, he was very cautious around his brothers having not been used to other children pulling out of him or robbing his toys at any opportunity. Now, his confidence was growing and it was so lovely watching our three boys playing together and building that special bond that I hoped they would carry through their lives forever. Brothers, such wonderful brothers.

Watching Freddie play and interact made us start to realize that the work we had put in around play in hospital with him was really standing to him. When Freddie had been stable in hospital, we had put a lot of time and effort into ensuring he received regular physio, occupational therapy and speech and language therapy so we could provide Freddie with as much positive early intervention therapy to help him thrive. We had heard from medical professionals and other parents of kids with Down Syndrome how important early intervention was and those three therapies were the key ones he needed initially. But another therapy that was available to us in the hospital that we hadn't heard about before was play therapy and its importance in the role of children in hospital. The charity that supported us with volunteers during our stay in hospital, *Children in Hospital Ireland*, were huge advocates for play therapy in hospital. They believe play is vitally important for children when they are in hospital; it provides a normalizing experience in a stressful situation, increasing their resilience and ability to cope with their illness. For children in hospital play is one of the few opportunities for them to have control over some aspect of their care.

We were incredibly grateful for their support during such a difficult time and could see firsthand that their beliefs were correct and that with the challenges we faced during our hospital stay we really understood how important play was, how much it stimulates and how much Freddie grew developmentally through play.

As I sat on the floor with all three boys reading books and stacking blocks it made my heart sing to see Freddie interact and join in. It was September and Freddie had just started sitting independently – something his physio said she didn't expect for him to do for at least another six months so you can imagine our delighted at watching him smash that milestone so soon after being home. I fully believed his rapid developmental growth was a direct result of being in his home environment and watching his brothers every move, eager to keep up.

The joy on his face as he experienced play outside of a hospital room and without wires connected to him was a simple pleasure I would never tire of relishing in. Play in hospital was certainly an escapism for Freddie, those moments were free from being poked and prodded by nurses and doctors. I believe Freddie had come to understand touch as being a negative thing – having bloods taken, being administered medication, blood pressure checks twice-daily and so forth but play was our way of showing him positive touch and interaction and watching him start to allow you guide his hand to block-stacking and page-turning made me thankful for these skills we learned while in hospital and how evident it was that Freddie responded so well to it.

Watching the boys play led my mind back to a study I read about when I was in hospital with Freddie, after he had been an inpatient for over six months; I was researching how such a long hospital admission might affect Freddie's mental health development. I came across a study completed by Ami Rokach of York University, Toronto and Walden University, Minesota that showed the experience of being hospitalized is usually an anxiety-provoking and even traumatic experience for children. When children are scared, tired or in pain they are particularly dependent on the safe and stable environment of their home and on the support and love of their family members in order to feel strength and capability. The research further showed that children's levels of physical activities are inherently limited in hospital and thus means their making sense of the world around them are threatened.

I knew there was nothing I could do when Freddie was sick, he needed to be in hospital and to be receiving medical care but I am thankful I was forward-thinking enough at the time to know such a long hospital stay couldn't *not* affect Freddie; I think it was because I was struggling so much with my own mental health during this time, I wondered could Freddie be affected by it also. From this, I tried to find ways that we could support him to minimize the long-lasting affects as much as possible and play therapy was just the support we needed to keep Freddie continuously learning and engaging whilst also making us, as Freddie's parents, feel like we were doing as much as we possibly could to give him the best possible start post-hospital. The play therapy sessions were not only of benefit to Freddie but to us also; the sessions were always so light-hearted and fun and took our minds off sickness, conversations with doctors and all the medical procedures; they injected some much-needed gentle relief during such a chaotic period in our lives.

Another thing that absolutely amazed me while undertaking research was the difference nature makes to children, particularly children that have been unwell. One day not long after Freddie came home, we walked to the local playground so Harry and Theo could play. Our local playground has a huge oak tree overshadowing it with its branches and leaves hanging down low. Freddie was absolutely in awe of the tree and took such joy and pleasure in watching the leaves blow to and fro and reaching his arms our to touch. It brought me to tears to think Freddie was denied this exposure having been confined to a hospital room for so long but I was elated to hear recently that the new Childrens hospital that is being built here in Dublin will have a huge emphasis on nature-therapy and has approximately 14 outdoor areas and gardens intertwined throughout the hospital to not only help children on their healing journeys but to encourage staffs' mental wellbeing also.

***

Come Halloween, we were starting to see some improvements in Freddie's health alongside his developmental progress. As Freddie was becoming stronger and now sitting independently, he would often pull his oxygen tube out – something that was always my biggest fear - but he did it so much and didn't have any immediate adverse reactions that it made us wonder if he really needed it as much as we thought he did? So, we started to do a few controlled experiments by taking his oxygen off and attaching him to a stats monitor to record his oxygen levels and what we discovered surprised us so much; he wasn't dropping in oxygen levels without the oxygen! Now, as non-medical professionals, it clearly wasn't our decision to remove him off oxygen, so instead we contacted his respiratory consultant Dr Carmine to ask her advice. She agreed it sounded positive but wanted us to do a study which would involve coming into the hospital to collect some equipment and attaching Freddie to it at home, this equipment would monitor all his vitals off the oxygen and send it remotely to the hospital. We did as she suggested and completed the home study at home a few weeks later. We knew it would take a further week or two to get the results so my heart skipped a beat when I saw Mae's office number calling me a few days later.

"I told Dr Carmine I wanted to be the one to call you. Freddie can come off oxygen," Mae said excitedly.

"What! Are you serious?!" I squealed in shocked delight.

"Yes, well done! This is such a huge milestone for you guys and I am so thrilled for you," Mae replied.

I broke down into a convulsion of tears after I got off the phone; big, huge, fat happy tears! These were the moments that made all the pain and heartache worth it. Seeing your child go through so much suffering and face so many challenges is gut-wrenching but when you see them overcome obstacles and do things you thought they might never do presents the most rewarding feeling.

Six months ago, we were told it might take Freddie four to five years to come off oxygen yet here we were six months later and he had smashed that goal. I couldn't have been prouder as I broke the news to Andrew who was just as relieved and thrilled as I was. We did it, we were doing it, and my gut told me this was only the beginning of positive change.

* * *

It was early December and having Freddie come off oxygen was the best early Christmas present we could have asked for. There had been a few hiccups since he had come home in July, we had three hospital admissions since then for minor respiratory infections where he needed that bit of extra support and some intravenous antibiotics but none of the stays lasted more than three nights. Making that initial decision that we needed to go to hospital and stepping through the hospital door was always the hardest part of those admissions; once we were there, we were always put at ease very quickly and admitted to our second home – St Peters ward. Seeing our friends on St. Peters was always the positive of having to stay in hospital, each time they were amazed at Freddie's progress and fussed over him like proud aunts and uncles.

On Christmas Eve, I was set to go to work for the day; we do Christmas catering as part of our offering with the business and it's a hugely busy time of year for us. I had done maybe two or three days at work over the last couple of months since Freddie came off oxygen. I didn't know if or when I would return to work but it was good for me to dip my toe back in a little and it was good for Freddie having some bonding time with his grandparents and aunts and uncles without myself or Andrew there.

I was looking forward to working today and soaking up some festive cheer with our team of staff and customers alike. As I was about to leave the boys with my mum, I could just tell Freddie wasn't 100% himself and was potentially brewing something; he was quiet and didn't want to be held or play which just wasn't like him.

"Please don't let him be sick for Christmas" I willed to myself.

I decided not to go to work and stay with the boys instead; in our experience with Freddie and illness things could escalate pretty quickly and I didn't want to put that pressure on my mum. However, as the day went on, I felt like Freddie was making a total liar out of me as he perked up and gave me the most joyous pose perched on a table in his elf onesie alongside Theo. My real-life elves-on-the-shelf.

"Maybe I was imagining this morning, maybe I am just so fearful of another Christmas spent away from home that I am seeing and feeling things that aren't really there," I said to Andrew that evening as I slumped into an exhausted sigh on the sofa.

"It's hard to forget everything we have been through but let's try being hopeful that this Christmas will be different. We've been through enough, we deserve this," Andrew replied softly.

We spent the rest of the evening trying to get the kids to bed which was a challenge tonight as a very excited four-year-old oozed excitement in anticipation for the big man's arrival.

"I have been so good this year mummy, Haven't I? Santy will bring me everything I want, won't he?" Harry asked in a desperate plea.

"You have been the best boy this year, Harry. I think Santy will be bringing you everything you asked for and you know what else?" I asked Harry.

"What Mummy?!" he replied as his head flew from his pillow into an upright position, eyes full of wonder.

"I think Santy might have an extra little surprise for you for being the best big brother ever!" I exclaimed; arms extended in gesture for a hug.

"I am so excited, Mummy!" Harry squealed as he embraced me tightly.

This was the first year me and Andrew had a child that truly understood the magic of Christmas and secretly we were just as giddy as Harry in anticipation for walking down the stairs the next morning.

* * *

"Mum, Dad! Wake up!" Harry shouted in glee as he jumped repeatedly on our bed. "I wonder if he's been yet!"

It was 6.30am. to be honest I was pleasantly surprised as I was full sure we might have a 4am wake-up call on our hands.

After we woke the twins, we walked down the stairs and headed for the sitting room.

"Look, look!" Harry roared as he pointed to Santa's snow-dusted boot marks that adorned our hallway.

"Oh, my goodness! He has been," I replied excitedly trying to match his infectious energy.

As we walked into the sitting room, Harry's eyes lit up as he saw his police motorbike accompanied by a police uniform and a police megaphone sitting centre-stage in the room. Harry was police obsessed and he was beside himself at the thought of getting to be a real policeman.

"Wow!" he cried in joy.

It wasn't long before Harry had us out the front door going up and down our cul-de-sac on his motorbike yelling "Merry Christmas" through his megaphone. As we completed our fifth lap, I hoped the neighbours without kids weren't cursing us from their beds.

"I want to call in for my friends!" Harry yelled as he biked his way into his best pal's driveway hammering the door to see what Santa had brought him. He was only four but Harry had built up some lovely little bonds with his pals. These friendships gave him some much-needed fun and distraction during some of our hardest periods; I was so thankful he had that.

After an hour outside in the freezing cold it was near-impossible to prize Harry away from his pals but the bike running out of charge was the catalyst that eventually got him to agree.

As we made our way back into the house and sat in front of a movie with our bacon sandwiches, I gave silent gratitude for being here; for getting to experience this magic morning with all my boys under one roof.

This was what it was all about.
Togetherness.
Family.
Health.
Nothing else matters; the presents, the Christmas decorations and the matching pyjamas the boys looked beyond adorable in were just the wonderful filler on this really special day.

* * *

As we continued to enjoy the festivities of Christmas Day with our extended family, it became clear to me that Freddie was really not well. His skin was pale, he was extremely cranky and he was working just that little bit too hard on his breathing.

"We need to bring him in," I told Andrew, as he was mid plating up dinner for nine people.

"Really, do you think so? Maybe give it a while, and see?" Andrew replied.

"No, we need to go now," I demanded.

After passing the most important meal of the year baton on to Andrew's brother Barry, we set off for the hospital.

"Whatever happens at least we had today, we got to see the boys enjoy Christmas morning. We got to see Harry so happy. I am so glad we had that," I whispered to Andrew as I sat in the back with Freddie rubbing his rosy, red cheek. I knew he would be okay but I also knew we would be staying in hospital for a few days, we were seasoned pros at this stage and we knew the drill.

After a long few hours in A&E, Freddie was put on oxygen to help with his breathing and we were moved to a ward. It wasn't St. Peters as there were no beds available but the nurses were just as kind. It always amazed me how nurses can remain so patient and kind when they are clearly so overwhelmed with the chaos that always seems to be present in hospital, especially during the winter months. They really are true earth angels and I hoped they knew just how much they were valued and appreciated by parents of sick children.

Once Freddie was settled in a room, I went home to the boys, leaving Andrew with Freddie. The house was eerily quiet as both the boys and Andrew's parents slept in that post-Christmas haze of exhaustion married with a food coma. As I climbed into my own bed, I cried soft sobs into my pillow as I reflected on the highs and lows that the last few days had brought. I always enjoyed the build-up to Christmas more than the day itself; soaking up the festive atmosphere around Dublin City, watching the Christmas lights being turned on lighting up the dullest of streets, cozy winter nights at home with hot chocolates, a festive candle lighting while watching Christmas movies as I wrapped presents. I was thankful we still had all of that this year, and with Freddie by our side too, but the sinking feeling that came with a hospital admission would always be there and I knew I would be holding my breath in some capacity until we had him home again.

* * *

When I woke the next morning and rang Andrew, I struggled to hear him with the bustle of commotion in the background.

"What's going on? Is everything okay?" I asked Andrew in a nervous panic.

"We are going to ICU," Andrew replied remorsefully.

"No! How? Why? Is he ok? Jesus, not again, we are passed this!" I cried.

"It's going to be okay, just get in when you can," Andrew said hurriedly as he ended the call.

After rallying family to look after the boys, I made my way to the hospital, boldly collecting some speeding penalty points en route. When I arrived at the first floor ICU unit, a place I was sure I would never see again, my stomach twisted. The smells, the sounds, the bright lights all doing their best to disguise themselves under the array of Christmas decorations that adorned every corner of the unit.

It is in this moment that I realised how much PTSD (post-traumatic stress disorder) I have. Being a mum to a child that is medically vulnerable and who has overcome so many obstacles allows so much space for hope, faith and positivity but it equally welcomes anxiety and fear on days like today. I have learnt being negative is a waste of energy but the feeling this hospital - particularly this unit - evokes in me requires me to use a lot of energy to stay grounded.

Walking into Freddie's room and seeing the painstaking familiarity of the ventilator and hand restraints made me shiver.

"Is he going to be okay?" I asked the ICU nurse on duty.

"He is quite poorly but we have everything under control and he is stable," she said matter-of-factly.

Stable. That is good. We need to hold onto that.

As the day passed and we sat by his bed, the doctor told us he had a bad respiratory infection that he was struggling with so much that the best course of action was to intubate to give his body and rest while he fights the infection. As I heard these words, these familiar words I had heard before, I could feel myself going down that dark hole I had been in before. Despair. Hopelessness. Anxiety.

"No, I don't want to feel this again," I said to myself.

I took myself off to the empty family room and I practiced my breathwork, an important tool from my toolkit when anxiety took hold. It would never cease to amaze me just how powerful the practice was and how quickly it can bring me from a ten back down to a one.

Everything was going to be okay; he was stable, this was a blip. We had come so far there was no way I was going to allow myself to be sucked back into that hole again. I needed to think positively. What I had learned about positive thinking during times of hardship over the last year had been of such huge benefit to me. I knew it was not about faking my feelings or pretending to be okay when I'm not; positive thinking is about trying to find any positivity I can in times of hardship. What is the lesson at the end of this challenge? What is the bigger picture here?

Freddie was stable; that was a positive.

We got to hospital before it escalated to an emergency situation at home; that was a positive.

We got to have a wonderful December and Christmas morning at home together; that was a positive.

Freddie is bigger, stronger and healthier than the last time he was in ICU; that was a positive.

We are stronger than we were last time he was in ICU; that was a positive.

I refused to let this admission break all the work I had done. Sure, ICU is a scary place and anything can happen in the blink of an eye but this time I chose to remain positive and I chose to hope for the best and I did my best to tune out any outside noise that could steer me otherwise.

We had this.

And we did have it, 10 days later Freddie came home and, apart from a few war-wounds from many cannula placements, he was back to his happy and joyful self like nothing had happened. Our warrior. Our miracle.

* * *

As we entered 2023, a new year full of hope and opportunity, I was certain I wanted to start the year on a positive note. I believed doing this would set the tone for how I wanted our year to go. I also wanted to give back in some way, to show my appreciation for the support, love and kindness we'd been shown for the past 18 months.

World Down Syndrome Day was also approaching on 21 March and I decided I would also like to do something to mark this day. Last year, Freddie was in hospital and the nurses made such a huge fuss of Freddie and celebrated him and the other children with Down Syndrome on the ward. I vowed to myself if Freddie was home this year, we would do our own celebration to make people feel the inclusion and positivity that was bestowed on us by the hospital staff that day.

With both of these thoughts playing heavily on my mind, I decided to run a fundraiser on World Down Syndrome Day to give back to The Down Syndrome Centre – and to help celebrate our peers in the Down Syndrome community with whom we had loved connecting and building relationships with. I wanted to see their kids celebrated as much as Freddie was last year.

Organizing the fundraiser brought me such joy; not only was I doing something that I felt so passionately about but it also gave me a taste of my work that I hadn't realized I had missed so much until now. Being able to use another side of my brain that wasn't in "mom-mode" was refreshing and I relished in having both *the babies and the business* again.

The night of the fundraiser soon came round. I had hired a function room in a local hotel and had 120 attendees supporting the night. Prior to the event I was so blown away by the level of support that came flooding in from the community in my hometown of Greystones; all of the local businesses I contacted sponsored tables and donated incredibly generous prizes to our raffle on the night. "How lucky Freddie was to be growing up in a town that supported acceptance and such inclusion?" I thought.

On the night I was so overcome with emotion giving an opening speech, I felt like the last 18 months of the rollercoaster of feelings came pouring out of me as I looked down over every person in the room who had been a part of our journey.

Our families who were our rocks and carried us through the hardest time in our lives,

Our friends, old and new, who were always there with a listening ear and a cup of tea,

Our wonderful Down Syndrome community peers with whom we walk this path with,

Jane and Holly, two of our most-loved nurses from Freddie's ward, who care so much and who we feel so incredibly blessed to now call friends.

This is what it is all about. This room were my tribe and by God what a tribe they were.

The night was more of a success than we could have ever anticipated and we raised over €18,000 for the Down Syndrome Centre. I was so incredibly proud of us for making this happen and I hoped Freddie and my other two boys would be proud one day too.

Finally, things felt like they were falling into place and I hoped that maybe we were approaching the start of the end of a very traumatic start to the completion of our family. We were certainly ready to start embracing a slower pace of life, soaking in the present, and starting to love this new joy-filled little life of ours.

Chapter 11

"Mum, Pixie is gone! Does that mean Santa has been?!" Harry asked as he shook me out of slumber at 4am. Pixie was Harry's elf-on-the-shelf who came for the month of December but went back to the North Pole with Santa on Christmas Eve. Truth be told, we would be happy to see the back of that bloody Elf; I have lost count of the number of nights myself and Andrew would climb into bed and suddenly realize the Elf needed to be moved and would bicker over who's turn it was to move it. Seeing the excitement in the boys' faces each morning as they looked for Pixie and the squeals out of them when they found him did make it worth it.

"Maybe Pixie is just helping Santa, it's still nighttime, we can't go in just yet," Andrew slurred after a late night of building toys.

"Ok, I will try go back to sleep," Harry shrugged sounding deflated.

"That's a good boy honey, only a few hours to go and you will see what's inside there," I whispered gesturing to the interconnecting sitting room.

"I can't wait!" Harry squealed as he shut his eyes tightly and eventually drifted back off to sleep.

Waking up this Christmas felt so different to this time last year. Although ending up in hospital last Christmas day came as somewhat of a shock; I think I knew in my gut on Christmas Eve that it was coming. But not this Christmas, this one we were staying together; I knew that with every fibre of my being.

We hadn't had a single hospital admission with Freddie since April; eight whole months without needing to go to hospital, it was a testament to how much Freddie had grown in strength and we were so proud of him. He was also now off all medications bar one. He was bum-shuffling everywhere and could now climb the stairs at lightning speed. 2023 had been a huge year of growth where life got that little bit lighter and a whole lot happier.

We knew it wouldn't be long before Freddie started walking and I knew the day that came would be a hugely emotional day for us all. There is something about a child taking those first steps that trumps all other milestones and I couldn't wait to see the pride of his face as he took those steps but there was also no rush; Freddie had shown us time and time again he will do everything he wants to do in his own time and that was just fine with us, we had all the time in the world.

We knew this year we needed to break the mould and I was determined not to live another December in fear of Christmas being hijacked by a hospital admission, so when Andrew's parents asked if we'd like to join them on a Christmas escape to a local hotel for three nights, we jumped at it. It was just the distraction we needed to have a goal to work towards and it was made even better by the fact that Andrew's brothers, partners and kids along with my mum and sister would be joining us – a proper family Christmas. A proper celebration.

"Bike! Bike!" Theo bellowed in excitement as he laid eyes on the yellow and red trikes Santa had left for himself and Freddie.

"My barber set! I got my barber set!" Harry squawked matching Theo's tone.

"Mama, Mama," Freddie said with his arms flailing in the air gesturing for me to pick him up and put him on the trike. He had only recently started saying mama and I can't tell you how warm it made my heart to hear it.

It was a beautiful morning watching all the boys immersed in the magic of Christmas and the hotel went to so much effort to ensure the magic was kept alive for the kids despite them not being in their own homes.

"Nana, Grandad! Come look at Santa's footprints!" Harry roared as he banged down the door of Beth and Paul's room.

The hotel adorned all the corridors with Santa's snow-dusted footprints and left remnants of carrots and cookies scattered outside bedroom doors. Harry and Theo were beside themselves with excitement. Theo really understood Christmas this year and himself and Harry riled each other up no end about who had been "the best boy" this year to receive the most presents. They would both sing "jingle bells" to Freddie every day without fail, which awarded them a bum-shuffling boogie from Freddie in return. They used to break their hearts laughing at him and his silly dance moves, which would only spur him on further. They were magic, those boys of ours.

After a morning spent playing with all their new toys and a dip in the pool, we enjoyed the most delicious meal.

"To health and having the boss here with us this year," Paul toasted as we all raised our glasses knowing the "boss" was indeed Freddie.

We were so lucky to all be here together, to be well and to see our boys so happy.

Harry spent most of the meal doing everyone's hair with his barber set in exchange for money; he was his father's son with his knack for business that was for sure! Theo would race through the corridor on his trike as Harry pushed Freddie along on his. Having all our family around us also meant myself and Andrew got to kick back a little at dinner and have a few drinks, something we hadn't done together in so long, usually having to socialize separately, neither one of us being confident leaving Freddie with family too long.

It was the perfect day and as I gave grateful thanks for getting to experience this reality, I took out my phone and made a donation online to the Children's Health Foundation, something I had decided to do every Christmas and on the twin's birthday each year, as a way of recognizing Freddie's first home and the importance of the work they do and the endless gratitude we will ALWAYS have to them for saving our boy.

As we slumped into an exhausted food-coma induced slumber that evening myself and Andrew toasted us for creating and giving our boys an amazing day. I knew these would be "the good old days" we would talk about in the future; the time we felt peace after the most turbulent two years.

* * *

Around the boys second birthday, last June, I went to see a life coach who lives local to me called Georgie Durcan. She has a holistic and soulful approach to how she guides you and I was so drawn to her from the minute I met her. After telling her everything I had been through, she asked me a question that changed everything.

"Take everything aside, the childcare and Freddie's needs. What do YOU want to do next?" Georgie asked.

"I want to go back to work. It's who I am," I told her defiantly. I had always believed that I'd be a working mum. My work, and our business, has always been so ingrained in my identity that I couldn't imagine a life without it.

"Okay, well then you need to do what you can to make this happen. Believe you will find the right person to mind the boys and take action to find that person. It will happen" she told me.

I had put my trust in the universe before and I could do it again. I didn't doubt that but I felt so protective over Freddie, he was still tube-fed with a language delay, so I would have to be 100% certain of a person before leaving the boys with them. Trust was of paramount importance to me and Andrew.

Before committing to my full return and finding a childminder for the boys, Andrew suggested trialling the experience. He'd spend a couple of days a week at home with the kids while I worked. So that's what we did and as a couple of weeks went by, I was deflated to realize I wasn't as happy back working as I had hoped. It wasn't filling that hole inside me that was screaming for attention. I found myself constantly checking up on the boys and wishing I was there when Andrew would send me pictures of them playing, dancing and reading books – that was my job.

I knew I had to dig deep on this and figure out why I wasn't satisfied so I decided to start journalling every day, something Georgie had recommended I do.

As I journalled each day that I hadn't wanted to be a stay-at home mum, that I was desperate to go back to work and claim my identity again, a thought suddenly dawned on me. It was like a flick had been switched and everything went from grey and dull to warm and bright.

My work is not my identity. It is not who I am.
I realize now that I had a narrative about who I was for so long that I never allowed myself to evolve. I was no longer the same person I was two years ago. I had changed, so it made sense that the narrative I held about myself needed to too.

My identity is no longer tied to my work. Right now, my purpose is to watch these boys grow up, with a full-time front-row seat. It makes me happy; I adore seeing my boys' building bonds and developing through play. I love being able to have conversations with Theo and teaching Freddie sign-language and watching him sign back. I love being there for Harry now that he's in junior school. I love being at those school gates when it's home-time and being the first person to hear all about his day.

Even though I had pushed against being a stay-at-home mum, it was because I believed I didn't have control over that decision. That it had been made for me, when the twins arrived and our lives were turned upside down. I felt I was a victim to it. So, I riled against it with all I had. But with this new realization, I realized that this was actually *my choice*. I realized that for so long I hadn't been craving my old life back, like I thought I had, I had been craving being in control of my own decisions.

Now, though, with this realization, I have control again and it's so empowering to realize that. Yes, life can be hard at times and sacrifices still have to be made, but this choice is not a sacrifice, it's what I want to do. My wants and desires have changed, and I've no doubt they will again, but next time, I know I won't be so reluctant to explore them.

* * *

One of the biggest lessons I've learnt in the last two years is that of balance. Yes, I am ok with being a stay-at-home mum, but that's not all of who I am. I know that I need to take care of me, Tracy, too. And I've built up a list of tools to use to do just that.

I sea-swim regularly and when I get down to the beach in the early morning before the kids wake it sets me up for the day like nothing else. The sea grounds me completely and I would be lost without her and her healing power.

I make sure I take time out at least once a week to see friends and just be "me", not a mother or wife or daughter, just me. My old friends and the new friends I have made in the Down Syndrome community are connections that mean so much to me and I enjoy my time out with them guilt-free, knowing I am a better mum having allowed myself that time. I am so lucky to have a small and tight friendship circle who not only love me and support me but adore my boys.

I work out twice a week in the gym. It can be really hard to fit that into my busy life but knowing the rush of energy I get post-workout makes it worth it and, knowing that I am doing it for *future-me* and the *future-mom* who wants to be able to keep up with her boisterous boys and set a strong example of looking after yourself mentally and physically, makes me feel like it's an essential non-negotiable for my life and well-being.

As well as the gym, I also recently took up running – and that is a sentence I never thought I would write! I used to look at people running and think "why?", walking was way more enjoyable in my opinion and I knew I would never be fit enough to run, but what led me to deciding to stick on those runners and download a "couch to 5k" programme was not so much about achieving a physical goal but more about achieving a mental one. You see, running to me seemed hard – like REALLY HARD – but I had proven to myself over the last couple of years that I can do hard things so why not try this? What had I to lose? The answer to that was nothing! If fact it is what I gained that surprised me most, I actually enjoyed running and I ran my first 5k after 8 weeks of building up my kilometres slowly.

* * *

Not only are our minds powerful, they are also incredibly smart. I fully believe my mind convinced me to distance myself, both physically and emotionally, from Freddie to protect my sanity. My mind knew I only had capacity for so much and so in turn it saved me from myself.

That teaching is probably the biggest thing I have learned on my journey and because of that I am now so passionate about minding my mental health and being aware of how my mind works.

In turn this made me realise just how important it is to instil mindfulness in kids young so they can carry this important skill through their life with them. So, you can imagine my delight when I met a fabulous woman called Jennie in my community who teaches weekly mindfulness practices to kids as young as five-years-old through the medium of crafting. Harry absolutely adores Jennie's classes, and Jennie herself.

Harry wouldn't talk much about the classes after I would collect him, I knew he enjoyed them which was lovely to see but my mind was soon to be blown at the realisation of just how much he got from these classes. During one of Freddies minor hospital admissions, Harry got really upset wondering how long Freddie would be in hospital - PTSD has a lot to answer for!

"Honey, Freddie is going to be just fine. He just needs to go and visit his nurse friends in the hospital and get some medicine and will be back to us real soon" I soothed my sobbing biggest little love.

"I know, mummy. I am just sad" Harry said as he placed a hand on his heart and started deep belly-breathing as his cries lessened.

"What are you doing, honey?" I asked gently as I observed him take breath after breath.

"Jennie says this is what to do when you want to feel calm" Harry assured me.

WOW.

"How incredible is it that my son, at the delicate ages of five, knows how to calm his nervous system? How beneficial is that going to be to him as he grows up?" I thought.

I gave silent gratitude for Jennie and the amazing work she is doing with our kids. I also congratulated myself on my teachings that allowed me to know I needed to seek out this practice for my kids to support their mental health as they grow up in this scary world.

Finally, everything we had been through was starting to make sense. I NEEDED to learn these teachings to give myself, and my family, the best and healthiest future possible.

* * *

Thanks to my life coach Georgie, I now attend my monthly "meditate and manifest" mornings, where a group of women who would spend the morning together sharing experiences and supporting each other, while being guided by Georgie. Each morning starts with some meditation and then we would get into deep-diving chats that would just flow. Never in my wildest dreams would I have seen myself attending these mornings but I was so drawn to Georgie's energy and trust her whole-heartedly.

What these mornings, and Georgie herself, have done for me is nothing short of life changing. The women I have met at these mornings are incredible. Sometimes we have laughed, sometimes we have cried but we have always held that space for each other. It was at one of these workshops that I opened up for the first time about wanting to write this book and the support I received once I spoke my truth brought me to tears.

Maternal mental health is something I feel incredibly passionate about now and, in my opinion, sharing your truth with other mothers, feeling seen and heard and also providing that same space in return is incredibly important and can be so healing. We are all the village and we must all look out for and empower each other.

After talking with another mum at one of the Georgie's mornings, who had also gone thorough having a child in hospital, we spoke about the NICU and how hard and lonely it can be. I went home with our conversation weighing heavily on my mind.

Why did it feel so lonely? It felt lonely because in the NICU we are in our own worlds, we are so consumed by the worry of our child that we don't see anything but the child in front of us, we're so consumed by our own pain. If I have learnt anything over the last two years it's the importance of talking, of connecting and supporting those who needed it *when* they needed it. With this in mind, I decided to do something completely out of my comfort zone that day, I wrote a poem about our experience of the NICU.

<u>Dear NICU Mama</u>
It was the eleventh Day of June when you rushed into the world,
Ten weeks too early all scrunched up and curled.
A brief kiss and a hug then off to NICU you were whirled,
The nurses now your protectors in this big outside world.
Little did we know how amazing those nurses were,
More like earth-angels – I'm sure you'll concur.
That time was hard as we contended with a lot,
Premmie twins, a diagnosis and tears that would not stop.
Night followed day as we sat by your cot,
Wondering how there was life before you – if there was, we forgot.
With a big brother at home desperate to say hello,
We willed you every day to thrive and grow.
We look at you now so boisterous and strong,
It's hard to believe we are home where we belong.
So, to all those earth-angels, thank you will never be enough,
You gave us so much strength when times were incredibly tough.
And to those currently navigating the NICU track,
I understand, sure, we are part of a pack.
My wish for you is that a day to come soon,
You'll be sat where I am after overcoming that time in June.

As if writing the poem wasn't far enough out of my comfort zone, I then decided to post it on Instagram. For some reason I just felt it needed to be shared. And I was right, because I was shocked by the responses I received.

Messages from those that had been through the same that felt seen.

Messages from friends in support of doing something they knew was so hard for me to do.

Tears from our family who felt every word written as they rode the journey with is.

Gratitude from people who said they had sent it on to friends or family currently in the NICU.

The power of connection will never cease to amaze me and I am so grateful to have learnt the art of connection.

* * *

My biggest, most important and most valued connection will always with Andrew and my three boys. Nurturing these relationships means more to me than anything else on this earth.

Andrew and I made huge sacrifices in our marriage in the last two years. There were times I wondered if we would make it and if the strain of the constant heartache and juggle would break us but we did make it. And we know valuing our marriage matters and making time for each other matters. It isn't always easy with three kids and a business but we are learning to take time out for date-nights and nights away just to be us again and remember who we were before having kids. We needed to heal as individuals but we also needed to heal together.

Andrew has always been the rock of our family and that hasn't come without a price. He has physically pulled me back together when I have fallen apart and has always shown-up and got stuck in with our kids even after a long and stressful day at work. He has felt the pressures and sacrifice of that by missing out of time with friends and minding his own self-care. He is taking longer than I am to realize it's okay to take time for yourself and mind yourself but he's getting there and for Andrew getting to continue to work on his business and his culinary creativity helps give him the headspace he needs too.

People often ask me is our family complete now. They ask would we like another child or "go for the girl" but my answer is always yes, we are most definitely complete. I feel so lucky to have my three boys and the yearning to have a girl isn't there. Our boys are all so different and have the most wonderful personalities.

Harry is my sensitive soul who feels everything so deeply. He is also the most sociable kid and is so clever to boot whilst also being the comedian of the family.

Theo is going to be the troublemaker of the family for sure! He oozes devilment and is completely fearless. He wins everyone over with his cheeky smile and I know he will be Freddie's biggest cheerleader as they get older.

Freddie is pure joy; he has the purest soul and adores music and dancing. It also goes without saying his strength knows no bounds. I know most people will fear having a child with additional needs, I know we did, but there really was no need. Yes, life is that bit more challenging living with a disability but his extra chromosome is the piece of the puzzle that completed our family. The lessons he has taught us will stay with us forever and I wouldn't change him, or his extra chromosome, for the world.

I look back on the day sat in the maternity hospital when I looked up those statistics about Down Syndrome and realising how much of a miracle it was that Freddie was here and hoping maybe one day I would see that. Well, I do see it now and my God I thank my lucky stars every day that he beat all those odds. We wouldn't be a family without him.

I used to also worry a lot about how our journey has impacted our boys. Would the two very turbulent years we had impact them mentally as they got older? Would they be anxious or fearful and would this stop them living fulfilled lives? These worries would cripple me a lot but recently I went for a reiki session and the fears I had around this came up but she then said something that changed everything for me. Here is what she said;

"Everyone arrives into this world exactly when they are supposed to and how they are supposed to. Anything they go through or experience are set in their life plan and we cannot control that. We are here to raise and guide our children but we cannot dictate their future and experiences and how they react to them."

Now I know to some this might sound a bit "woo" but for me it did something to me that made me feel physically lighter. It was freeing. I realise I cannot control what happened and I absolutely did my best - and continue to do my best - and that's good enough. I am good enough.

And as for me and what's next in my story? Well, that's still very much unwritten and guided by my boys for now but what I do know is that I will use this experience to help other people.

I did look into going back to college to train in perinatal mental health but right now that seems like too big a challenge to take on with three young children. Instead, inspired by a mothers circle I attended recently ran by a wonderful woman named Lucy, I am currently training to be a mothers circle facilitator.

Mothers' circles are still relatively unheard of but they involve bringing mums together in a circle to share, talk, laugh or cry in a non-judgemental and safe space. I found Lucys circle incredibly moving and healing, there is so much to be said just sharing space with like-minded women who hold no judgement and allow you to speak your truth. It might not be traditional therapy and I won't have all the answers but there is a lot to be said for that connection and shared experience and I believe mums need so much more of that. My hope would be to bring these circles to NICU and Childrens hospitals helping mums who need that added support and connection during hard times.

I recently read a quote that J.K Rowling said during her Harvard Commencement Address in 2008 in which she said *"The strength of a mother is the foundation on which a family thrives"* and I feel that says it all. Our children mean the world to us, we would do anything to ensure their health, wellbeing and safety but that starts with us. We matter just as much - and may we never forget it.

About the Author

Tracy Holmes is a devoted mother of three, residing in the picturesque setting of Co. Wicklow, Ireland. Since embarking on her work life at the age of 15, Tracy has developed a passion for food retail, climbing the ranks within a prestigious food establishment before co-founding her own catering business with her husband, Andrew, in 2013.

Though career-driven and fiercely independent, Tracy's life took an unexpected turn with the birth of her twins in 2021. Born prematurely, one of her twins required extensive medical care, spending his first year in hospital. The postnatal diagnosis of Down Syndrome and the subsequent challenges prompted Tracy to reassess her priorities and values.

Now, in 2024, Tracy and her family enjoy a contented life in Greystones. Her experience as a mother to a child with additional needs has brought its share of fears and anxieties, but it has also revealed moments of joy and hope. Tracy is committed to sharing the positive aspects of her journey with others.

Motivated by her personal battles, including overcoming a postnatal mental health crisis in 2021, Tracy has penned a book to share her story. She believes her experiences offer valuable insights for other women facing similar challenges, providing inspiration and support in their own journeys.

Please Review

Dear Reader,

I would deeply appreciate if you would spread the word about this publication. As a first-time author, your support can make a significant difference to helping my book get found by those who would be most interested in my story and help others find my book. Thank you. - Tracy

Acknowledgements

To Andrew. Thank you for being on this journey with me and being the greatest dad to our boys and looking after us all how you do. It's been a rollercoaster but we survived it and I am so proud of us.

To my boys. One day, when you have your own children, you'll come to understand the unconditional love we have for the three of you. You make us so proud every day and bring so much joy to our lives. As we say every night at bedtime – "You are in my heart".

To our families – you all know who you are. Words will never be enough to thank you for the sacrifices you made to support us in our darkest hours. We genuinely don't know where we would be today without our incredible village which is all of you. Our boys will never be allowed to forget just how much their grandparents, aunts and uncles love and cherish them.

To our friends – again you all know who you are. Thank you for the support, kindness and, above all else, friendship during the hardest time of our lives. Spending time with you allowed us to just be "us" and not "mum and dad". Here's to many more years of friendship, good times and supporting one another.

To my writing coach Elaine O'Neill. Thank you for believing in my story and holding me accountable - especially during the hard parts. This book wouldn't exist without you and I am so happy to have met you and benefitted from your amazing talent.

To my publisher Orla Kelly. Thank you for being on this journey with me, for believing in "Raising Resilience" as much as I do and for your constant expertise and guidance.

To all the doctors, midwives, sonographers, therapists and general staff in The National Maternity Hospital and Crumlin Children's Hospital. Thank you for doing the job you do; you are all real-life earth angels and you literally transitioned our twin boys from just surviving to thriving whilst supporting us too. Thank you just does not seem enough so please know you are so appreciated and we will be forever grateful.

To The Jack and Jill Foundation. What incredible work you do! You not only supported us when we were on our knees in hospital but you supported us so much when our journey started at home. Knowing we had nurses to help us with our vulnerable baby when he first came home allowed us space to breathe again. Particular thanks and gratitude must go to our family co-ordinator Fiona and our incredible nurses, in and out, of hospital – Orla, Jane, Holly, Niamh and Lucy.

To Children in Hospital Ireland (CIH). The work you do is so incredibly impactful and important. It saddens me a little to know most people will be unaware of who you are until they, or someone they know, needs you. We will never stop shouting your name and encouraging support for the amazing work you do. Thank you.

To the Homecare team and are our incredible co-ordinator Aisling. Thank you for always listening to and supporting us. Our first months' home with Freddie were made so much easier with your support. A special thank you must go to our wonderful night-nurse Sheila – thank you for the love, support and late-night chats!

To The Down Syndrome Centre. What can I say? The education, support, guidance, positivity, inclusion and the general "can do" attitude we felt and learned from you since the first day we stepped through your door has not waivered. The friends and connections we have made will be lifelong and the therapies and classes you provide for babies, children and young adults with Down Syndrome is second to none. We feel so incredibly lucky to have the centre in our corner and look forward to many more years with you.

To the amazing women in my community and in the Down Syndrome community who have lifted me up and supported myself and my family in some way, thank you. You are all part of the reason I get to sit here and write this today. It's true what they say – when women support women amazing things happen. I look forward to many more years of support, connection and empowerment.

Finally, to all the mums out there. Being a mum is the hardest and most challenging thing I have ever done so I applaud each and every one of you. The pressure on mothers in this day and age is huge and the mental load of holding it all together, all the time, is challenging. Just know you are enough and when you worry about being a good enough mum it just means you already are one.

Printed in Great Britain
by Amazon